Development Lead · Owen K.C. Stephens
Authors · Alexander Augunas, Steven T. Helt,
  Luis Loza, and Ron Lundeen
Cover Artist · Kiki Moch Rizky
Interior Artists · Melvin Chan, Marjorie Davis,
  Tawny Fritzinger, Lance Red, and Anson Tan

Editor-in-Chief · F. Wesley Schneider
Creative Director · James Jacobs
Executive Editor · James L. Sutter
Senior Developer · Rob McCreary
Developers · John Compton, Adam Daigle,
  Mark Moreland, and Owen K.C. Stephens
Assistant Developers · Crystal Frasier,
  Amanda Hamon Kunz, and Linda Zayas-Palmer
Senior Editors · Judy Bauer and Christopher Carey
Editors · Jason Keeley and Josh Vogt
Lead Designer · Jason Bulmahn
Designers · Logan Bonner, Stephen Radney-MacFarland,
  and Mark Seifter

Managing Art Director · Sarah E. Robinson
Art Director · Sonja Morris
Senior Graphic Designer · Adam Vick
Graphic Designer · Emily Crowell

Publisher · Erik Mona
Paizo CEO · Lisa Stevens
Chief Operations Officer · Jeffrey Alvarez
Director of Sales · Pierce Watters
Sales Associate · Cosmo Eisele
Marketing Director · Jenny Bendel
Vice President of Finance · Christopher Self
Staff Accountant · Ashley Kaprielian
Data Entry Clerk · B. Scott Keim
Chief Technical Officer · Vic Wertz
Software Development Manager · Cort Odekirk
Senior Software Developer · Gary Teter
Project Manager · Jessica Price
Organized Play Coordinator · Tonya Woldridge
Adventure Card Game Designer · Tanis O'Connor

Community Team · Liz Courts and Chris Lambertz
Customer Service Team · Sharaya Copas,
  Katina Davis, Sara Marie Teter, and Diego Valdez
Warehouse Team · Will Chase, Mika Hawkins,
  Heather Payne, Jeff Strand, and Kevin Underwood
Website Team · Christopher Anthony, Lissa Guillet,
  Julie Iaccarino, Erik Keith, and Scott Spalding

On the Cover

Artist Kiki Moch Rizky brings us two drow warriors getting the drop on a well-equipped seugathi in the Darklands on this amazing cover.

Table of Contents

Introduction	2
The Taint of Shadow	4
Transformed by Shadow	6
Transformed by Light	10
Transformed by the Darklands	14
Shadowy Archetypes	18
Fighting in the Dark	20
Shadowcraft Weapons	22
Shadow Feats	24
Shadow Magic Items	26
Penumbral Spells	28
Shadow Spells	30
Illumination Levels	Inside Front Cover

Reference

This Pathfinder Player Companion refers to several other Pathfinder Roleplaying Game products and uses the following abbreviations. These books are not required to make use of this Player Companion. Readers interested in references to Pathfinder RPG hardcovers can find the complete rules from these books available for free online at **paizo.com/prd**.

Advanced Class Guide	ACG	*Pathfinder Unchained*	PU
Advanced Player's Guide	APG	*Ultimate Combat*	UC
Advanced Race Guide	ARG	*Ultimate Equipment*	UE
Occult Adventures	OA	*Ultimate Magic*	UM

Paizo Inc.
7120 185th Ave NE, Ste 120
Redmond, WA 98052-0577

paizo.com

Introduction

Darkness always lurks just beyond the reach of the light. Lightlessness is the natural state of the universe, held briefly at bay by fire, moonlight, magic, or pale torches held in trembling hands. While most of the surface world enjoys many hours of sunlight each day, vast regions exist far below, where natural light never reaches. The Darklands' huge caverns and countless tunnels stretch untold distances around Golarion; within them, entire empires have grown in endless gloom and permanent night.

In addition to the unlit places on the Material Plane, the Shadow Plane lurks just out of sight. Coterminous and coexistent with the Material Plane, this colorless reality is populated by twilight analogs of the mortal world and, in some cases, even contains shadowy equivalents of great cities, including Absalom. The Shadow Plane has its own natural gray terrain, such as caves, mountains, and forest floors, all parts of a dim world with unique native denizens, threats, politics, and even economic needs. While most of those who dwell on Golarion would never guess that an additional world, with its own great cities and ancient empires, overlays their own reality within the shadows, there are others who deal regularly with visitors from the Shadow Plane, hoping to advance trade, intrigue, or power.

Characters influenced by shadow can make for some of the most exciting stories. Inherent in any tale of light and darkness are the spaces between, filled with limitless potential. From the literal shadows where assassins skulk and undead drain strength, to the veil of secret knowledge sought by scholars and roaming vagabonds in the deep places of the world, darkness influences the destiny of those both above- and belowground. Supernatural forces and strange energies combine to alter those who travel the Shadow Plane and the cavernous Darklands into darker versions of themselves. Over generations, even kingdoms of the long-lived elves and dwarves have been changed by their exposure to forces that dwell only in the lightless places. *Blood of Shadows* presents rules for characters born or changed by the shadows, and the power that darkness provides.

Shadow Origins

Over passing ages, countless souls have ventured into dark places of danger and opportunity. Some hail from Nidal, a nation dominated by lords from the umbral reaches. Others have strong ties to the Shadow Plane, the long-abandoned home plane of the wayangs who now dwell in the Dragon Empires, and the current residence of the fetchlings who fled there from doomed Azlant. Some find themselves fleeing into the Darklands to avoid threats of the surface world, or trying to escape its eternal murk in hopes of seeing the sky at least once. Though drow, fetchling, and wayang characters have obvious ties to dark places, there are a number of possible ways other characters' origins could be tied to the powers of shadow, such as those presented below.

Benign Envoy

Settlements in the Darklands that resist the corrupting taint to which their neighbors long ago succumbed sometimes brave the journey to the surface to establish trade and recruit allies. An emissary from the lightless reaches requires time to adjust to life under the sun. Luckily, such characters don't tend to carry the arrogance or hostility present in the evil denizens of the Darklands.

Child of Shadow

Born into a twilight realm, many shadow-tainted creatures know little of bright daylight or subterranean darkness. They dwell in the alleys between tall buildings or among the thick trees of dense forests, avoiding the discomfort of bright light, even though it might be only the toss of a dagger away. Their survival depends on the ability to hide and scavenge, and these children of the shadow know no other way.

Hiding from the Light

It isn't uncommon for one to flee from abuse or persecution. Whether a criminal or a victim, such fugitives abandon a normal life in order to remain free from the law or their tormentor. These individuals practice stealth and live beneath the notice of their neighbors, using magic or guile to keep their secrets from coming to light.

Liberated Laborer

Though the surface world has its share of nations that indulge in slavery, the Darklands are full of chattel captured from both surface settlements and subterranean cities. Those who manage to free themselves from bondage fight to reach the surface, or at least find a community belowground that doesn't think of them as property.

Trapped by Terror

The nation of Nidal conditions the majority of its citizens to live amid cruelty and supernatural horror. Though few opportunities to escape the darkness shrouding that land occur, they are not outside the realm of possibility. Adventurers, traveling musicians, political envoys, and trade emissaries can still serve their homeland loyally, but from a position far removed from the persistent gloom in which they were raised.

Umbral Operative

There are those who serve the shadow directly; agents of kingdoms on the Shadow Plane or divine servants of Zon-Kuthon often work in obscurity to eclipse light and warmth. While not all umbral operatives are evil, their allegiance to shadow certainly colors their actions and attitudes. Their presence heralds a coming darkness that threatens to envelop everyone around them.

Rules Index

The following new rules options are located on the indicated pages, alongside several other options.

ARCHETYPES	CLASS	PAGE
Dusk knight	Paladin	18
Gloom chymist	Alchemist	18
Shadow walker	Rogue	9
Umbral scion	Sorcerer	19

FEATS	TYPE	PAGE
Blinded Blade Style	Combat, Style	24
Blinded Competence	Combat	24
Blinded Master	Combat	24
Cloak and Dagger Style	Combat, Style	24
Cloak and Dagger Subterfuge	Combat	25
Cloak and Dagger Tactics	Combat	25
Crepuscular Cowl	—	7
Drow Spirit	—	15
Eclipsed Spell	Metamagic	25
Extra Light and Dark	—	11
Extra Ninja Trick	—	25
Extra Shadow Jump	—	25
Flexible Shadow Jump	—	25
Improved Shadowy Resistance	—	7
Shadow Magic Defense	—	7
Snuffing Spell	Metamagic	25
Surface Scout	—	15
Wayang Soothsayer	—	11

OTHER RULES OPTIONS	PAGE
Advanced rogue talents	8
Darkborn alternate racial traits	5
Drow alternate racial traits	14
Drow favored class options	15
Drow spells	15
Fetchling alternate racial traits	6
Fetchling favored class options	6
Half-elf alternate racial traits	14
Illumination magic items	21
Penumbral spells	28
Rogue talents	7
Shadow blessing (warpriest blessing)	17
Shadow (bloodrager bloodline)	16
Shadow eidolon (unchained summoner)	11
Shadow ink tattoos	12
Shadow magic items	26
Shadow (oracle mystery)	12
Shadow (psychic discipline)	17
Shadow spells	30
Shadow subdomain (cleric subdomain)	17
Shadowborn alternate racial traits	4
Shadowcraft weapons	22
Wayang alternate racial traits	10
Wayang favored class options	10
Wayang spells	11

The Taint of Shadow

To those who live in the light, using candles and hearths to keep darkness at bay even when sleeping, night and shadow are often symbols of danger and depravity. Despite civilization's best efforts, the influence of magical shadow fills every darkened corner of Golarion, and is a gateway to illusion, necromancy, and the spiritual presence of unknowable beings. While those who dwell in the shadows are not necessarily evil, many succumb to corruption, whether clerics and oracles worshiping the Outer Gods, drow serving demon lords, or witches gaining power from dark patrons.

The following racial traits can be found among those creatures with family trees rooted in the shadows, or who gain power from lives lived away from the light.

Shadowborn Alternate Racial Traits

The influence of shadow alters those it touches, from individuals to entire races. For some, the transition occurs naturally over generations, due to environmental factors or exposure to dark energies. For others, it manifests after a single magical event. In very rare cases, these powers are the result of a shadowy ancestor of a different species.

A character with such a background can select one or more shadowborn racial traits. Such racial traits replace one or more normal racial traits for the character's race. If you are using the race builder rules from *Pathfinder RPG Advanced Race Guide*, the Race Point (RP) cost for each

shadowborn racial trait is given. Otherwise, each trait lists the racial trait it replaces if taken by certain characters of the eight core races.

Behind the Veil (1 RP): Characters with this trait slyly cover their body language and movements by acting in a shadowed or partitioned areas. These characters gain a +2 bonus on Bluff and Sleight of Hand checks while benefiting from concealment or cover.

Dwarves can take this trait in place of stonecunning. Elves, gnomes, and half-elves can take this trait in place of low-light vision. Half-orcs can take this trait in place of intimidating, also gaining the shadow blending^{ARG} fetchling racial trait. Halflings can take this trait in place of weapon familiarity.

Dimdweller (2 RP): Characters with this trait are at home in gloomy conditions. Whenever these characters benefit from concealment or full concealment due to darkness or dim light, they gain a +2 racial bonus on Intimidate, Perception, and Stealth checks.

Dwarves can take this trait in place of the greed and stonecunning traits. Elves, gnomes, halflings, and half-orcs can take this trait in place of weapon familiarity. Half-elves can take this trait in place of adaptability. Humans can take this trait in place of the skilled trait, also gaining darkvision to a range of 60 feet.

Dusksight (2 RP): Characters who operate below canopies or fight in dimly lit caves and shadowy planes of existence learn to use their low-light vision to deduce a foe's position from the flickers of shadows around a target. When making ranged attacks, characters with this trait can reroll the miss chance granted by cover to any target in dim light, and take the better of the two rolls. The miss chance for total concealment applies normally.

Dwarves can take this trait in place of hatred and darkvision, also gaining low-light vision. Elves, gnomes, half-elves, and halflings can take this trait in place of keen senses. Half-orcs can take this trait in place of weapon familiarity, also gaining low-light vision.

Shadowhunter (2 RP): Those who understand the connection between shadows and the Negative Energy Plane know how to fight the spirits of darkness. Characters with this trait deal 50% weapon damage to incorporeal creatures when using nonmagical weapons (including natural and unarmed attacks), as if using magic weapons. They also gain a +2 bonus on saving throws to remove negative levels, and recover physical ability damage from attacks by undead creatures at a rate of 2 points per ability score per day (rather than the normal 1 point per ability score per day).

Dwarves, elves, gnomes, half-orcs, and halflings can take this trait in place of weapon familiarity. Half-elves can take this trait in place of elven immunities. Humans can take this trait in place of their bonus feat, also gaining Iron Will as a bonus feat.

Shadowplay (1 RP): Some illusionists are experts in manipulating light and darkness. Characters with this trait cast spells with the darkness, light, or shadow^UM descriptor at +1 caster level.

Dwarves can take this trait in place of greed. Elves can take this trait in place of elven magic, also gaining the fetchling's spell-like abilities^ARG racial trait. Gnomes can take this trait in place of gnome magic. Halflings can take this trait in place of weapon familiarity. Half-orcs can take this trait in place of intimidating, also gaining the gnome's illusion resistance racial trait.

Darkborn Alternate Racial Traits

Those entirely deprived of light survive the eclipse by embracing the darkness in their homes, and often in their souls. As a result, darkborn traits are sometimes found in creatures who can trace their heritage back to drow cities. Some of these darkborn are rare half-drow elves or half-elves who have both drow and non-drow blood coursing through their veins as a result of either unusual parentage or some form of heritage-blending experimentation. Others are descendants of slaves exposed to demonic rituals, necromantic fleshcrafting, or occult influences. The darkness of Rovagug himself, chained in the planet's heart, sometimes seeps into the bloodlines of those who dwell in the wrong caverns for generations.

Darkborn racial traits are presented similarly to the shadowborn traits found above, but not every race has a strong enough connection to the darkness to be eligible for them. Some of these traits even have prerequisites of other racial traits or ability scores.

Blended View (2RP): *Prerequisite:* low-light vision. Half-drow whose non-drow parent had low-light vision might be blessed with a legacy of versatile senses. Characters with this trait keep their low-light vision but also gain darkvision to a distance of 60 feet.

Elves or gnome can take this trait in place of keen senses. Half-elves can take this trait in place of multitalented.

Darklands Guide (2 RP): Those who brave the lightless tunnels below Golarion's surface learn to identify the dangerous phenomena that characterize the Darklands. Characters with this trait gain a +2 bonus on initiative checks, and on saves against traps and hazards when underground (from a lifetime of dodging accursed pools, cave-ins, and green slime).

Drow and half-elves can take this trait in place of keen senses. Tieflings can take this trait in place of the *darkness* spell-like ability.

Poison Minion (4 RP): Drow sometimes augment their slaves and frontline warriors by making them toxic, causing their bodies to internally produce mawbane poison (see below). The resulting poisonous creature makes a potent weapon in the effort to discourage neighboring monsters. Any creature that hits such a character with a bite attack is immediately exposed to its poison. The save DC for this poison is equal to 10 + 1/2 the character's Hit Dice + the character's Constitution modifier.

Mawbane Poison—ingested; *save* Fortitude as above; *frequency* 1/round for 4 rounds; *effect* 1d2 Constitution damage; *cure* 1 save.

Dwarves can take this trait in place of defensive training and hardy. Elves can take this trait in place of elven magic and weapon familiarity. Gnomes can take this trait in place of defensive training, gnome magic, and illusion resistance. Half-elves can take this trait in place of elven immunities and keen senses. Half-orcs can take this trait in place of orc ferocity and weapon familiarity. Humans can take this trait in place of skilled. Halfling physiology prevents them from taking this trait. Drow can take this trait in place of drow immunities, light blindness, spell resistance, and weapon familiarity. Wayangs can take this trait in place of light and dark, lurker, and shadow resistance.

Sure Step (2 RP): Adventurers can spend their whole careers in the alleys and sewers of large cities or the tunnels of the Darklands. Characters with this trait suffer no movement penalties when blinded or moving in darkness.

Drow and half-elves can take this trait in place of keen senses.

Voice in the Darkness (2 RP): *Prerequisite:* Charisma 13+. Characters who practice coercion and intimidation in the Darklands or on the Shadow Plane learn to do so in dim light or no light at all. As long as they are in dim light or darker conditions, characters with this trait gain a +2 bonus on Intimidate and Stealth checks.

Dwarves can take this trait in place of stonecunning. Drow and elves can take this trait in place of weapon familiarity. Half-elves can take this trait in place of adaptability. Half-orcs can take this trait in place of intimidating.

Transformed by Shadow

As the Azlanti saw their sky fill with the meteors that portended the cataclysm of Earthfall, some of them accepted an offer of salvation from an inscrutable being known as the Widow. Fleeing through a rift the Widow opened into the Shadow Plane, these humans were indeed saved—but they were also trapped. Over generations, the refugees adapted to and were altered by their new home, becoming the colorless, gaunt humanoids called fetchlings. Most races native to the Material Plane seem to sense fetchlings' otherworldly nature, and they often regard fetchlings as eerie and alien creatures of shadow. The pragmatic fetchlings are happy to use this perception to their advantage.

Over subsequent millennia, many fetchlings have mastered planar travel and occasionally return to the Material Plane, making excursions to experience the vibrant colors and music that are so rare in their umbral home. Some fetchlings have emigrated back to Golarion, although they often have trouble blending in on their old homeworld. A small minority of fetchlings exists in most large cities, but there are two major population concentrations on the Material Plane. One is in Nidal, where they live as an underclass on the margins of society, mistrusted and feared. The other is in Absalom, where they often carry trade between the City at the Center of the World and Shadow Absalom, the great metropolis found in the same location on the Shadow Plane.

Fetchling Alternate Racial Traits

The following racial traits can be selected instead of existing fetchling racial traits. Consult your GM before selecting any of these new options.

Bound to Golarion: Some Nidalese fetchlings are from families that have fearfully avoided the Shadow Plane, living on Golarion for generations. As a result, these fetchlings are closely tied to the Material Plane. Fetchlings with this racial trait count as outsiders with the native subtype and humanoids with the human subtype for any effect related to race, including feat prerequisites and spells that affect humanoids. They can pass for human without using the Disguise skill. This racial trait replaces the +2 racial bonus on Knowledge (planes) checks from the skilled racial trait, and alters the native outsider racial trait.

Boundary Walker: Fetchlings of Absalom and Shadow Absalom deftly navigate between the worlds of shadow and light. A fetchling with this racial trait gains spell resistance equal to 5 + his character level against spells and spell-like abilities with the light or shadow descriptors, as well as spells and spell-like abilities of the illusion (shadow) subschool. This racial trait replaces the shadow blending and shadowy resistance racial traits.

Deep Shadow Explorer: Fetchlings who widely explore the Shadow Plane learn to confront fearsome things best left undescribed. Fetchlings with this racial trait gain a +2 racial bonus on all saves against fear effects. This racial trait replaces the skilled racial trait.

Nidalese Recluse: Some fetchlings learn how to deflect unwanted attention. Fetchlings with this racial trait can use *sanctuary* once per day as a spell-like ability. When such a fetchling reaches 9th level in any combination of classes, he gains *nondetection* (self only) as a spell-like ability usable once per day, and at 13th level, he gains *veil* (self only) usable once per day. A fetchling's caster level is equal to his total Hit Dice. This racial trait modifies the fetchling's spell-like abilities racial trait.

Umbral Escort: Some fetchlings descend from talented planar travelers who dwelled in the dark places between worlds and could conduct others across the planes. A fetchling with this racial trait loses the *disguise self* spell-like ability, but his *shadow walk* and *plane shift* spell-like abilities need not affect himself only. This racial trait replaces the low-light vision racial trait and modifies the spell-like abilities racial trait.

Whispers from Shadow: Fetchlings from Absalom are known for wheeling and dealing from the city's shadows. A fetchling with this racial trait gains a +4 racial bonus on Bluff checks when he tells a lie and wants to convince an opponent that what he is saying is true. This racial trait replaces the skilled racial trait.

Fetchling Favored Class Options

The following options are available to all fetchlings who have the listed favored class. They supplement the options found in the *Pathfinder RPG Advanced Race Guide*. Unless otherwise stated, the bonus applies each time you select the favored class reward.

Alchemist: Add +1 to Craft (alchemy) checks to craft poison and +1/4 to the DCs of poisons the alchemist creates.

Arcanist: When the arcanist casts an illusion (shadow) spell that deals a percentage of its damage or effect against nonbelievers, increase this amount by 2% (to a maximum of 100%).

Barbarian: Add +1 to either cold or electricity resistance while raging (maximum resistance 15 for either type).

Bard: Add a +1 bonus on Disguise checks when using *disguise self*.

Cleric: Add 1/2 point to negative energy damage dealt by channeling energy and *inflict wounds* spells.

Druid: The druid's animal companion gains resistance 1 against either cold or electricity. Each time the druid selects this reward, he increases his animal companion's resistance to one of those energy types by 1 (maximum 10 for any one energy type). If the druid ever replaces his animal companion, the new animal companion gains these resistances.

Fighter: Choose a slashing melee weapon. Add +1/2 to critical hit confirmation rolls made while using that weapon (maximum bonus of +4). This bonus does not stack with Critical Focus.

Gunslinger: Add 1/4 point to the gunslinger's grit.

Hunter: The hunter's animal companion gains DR 1/magic. Each additional time the hunter selects this benefit, the DR increases by +1/2 (maximum DR 10/magic). If the hunter ever replaces his animal companion, the new animal companion gains this DR.

Inquisitor: Add a +1 bonus on Knowledge (planes) checks made to identify creatures.

Magus: Add 1/4 point to the magus's arcane pool.

Monk: Add a +1/2 bonus on Escape Artist and Stealth checks attempted while in dim light or darkness.

Paladin: Add +1/4 to the morale bonus the paladin grants on allies' saving throws against fear effects.

Slayer: Add a +1/4 dodge bonus to Armor Class against the slayer's studied target.

Shadowy Feats

The following new feats are favored by fetchlings and other characters that dwell in the shadows.

Crepuscular Cowl

Your affinity with the Shadow Plane allows you to draw a cloak of concealing gloom around you, even in bright light.

Prerequisites: Stealth 9 ranks, shadow blending racial trait or shadow call shadowdancer prestige class feature.

Benefit: As a swift action, you can pull a haze of shadow around you, granting yourself concealment (20% miss chance) in bright light or normal light for 1 minute. You can use this ability once per day, plus one additional time per day when your character level reaches 12th, 15th, and 18th.

Improved Shadowy Resistance

You have developed a resistance to the life-sapping environment of the Shadow Plane.

Prerequisites: Fetchling, shadowy resistance racial trait.

Benefit: You gain resistance 5 against negative energy damage, do not lose hit points when you gain a negative level, and gain a +2 racial bonus on saving throws against death effects, energy drain, negative energy, and spells or spell-like abilities of the necromancy school.

Shadow Magic Defense

Your mastery of shadow allows you to defend against shadow magic used against you.

Prerequisite: *Disguise self* racial spell-like ability or shadow illusion shadowdancer prestige class feature.

Benefit: You gain a +2 bonus on saving throws against spells and spell-like abilities with the shadow[UM] descriptor or spells and spell-like abilities of the illusion (shadow) subschool. If you succeed at a saving throw against an illusion (shadow) spell that deals a percentage of its damage or effect against creatures that successfully save against it, reduce the amount of damage it deals to you by 20% (to a minimum of 0%).

Other Character Options

The following options particularly appeal to fetchlings, but are available to any characters who meet the requirements and are interested in dabbling with shadow.

Rogue Talents

Although the new talents presented below are common among fetchlings, any character who can take rogue talents (including rogues, shadowdancers, and unchained rogues[PU]) and who meets the prerequisites can take any of these talents. Slayers[ACG] can also take these talents as if they were slayer talents. When one of these talents indicates a benefit based on the rogue's level, it provides that benefit based on the character's level in the class that granted that rogue talent. A character cannot take a talent more than once, unless the talent states otherwise. If a character's class offers a talent with the same name as one of these talents (such as slayers and the poison use slayer talent), the character cannot take the relevant talent listed here . Talents marked with an asterisk (*) add effects to a character's sneak attack. Only one of these talents can be applied to an individual attack, and the decision must be made before the roll is made. A character lacking the sneak attack class feature cannot select these talents.

Cloying Shades (Su): When a rogue with this talent uses *dimension door* as a spell or spell-like ability, including the abundant step or shadow jump class feature, then all creatures adjacent to the rogue at the start and end of her teleportation are entangled by grasping shadows for 1 round (although the creatures are not anchored in place). A successful Reflex saving throw negates this effect. The DC of this saving throw is equal to 10 + 1/2 the rogue's level + the rogue's Intelligence or Charisma modifier (whichever is higher). The rogue must have *dimension door* as a spell or spell-like ability (including the abundant step or shadow jump class feature) before choosing this talent.

Emboldening Strike* (Ex): When a rogue with this talent hits a creature with a melee attack that deals sneak attack damage, she gains a +1 circumstance bonus on saving throws for every 2 sneak attack dice rolled (minimum +1) for 1 round.

Extinguishing Strike* (Ex): When a rogue with this talent hits a creature with a melee attack that deals sneak attack damage, any nonmagical light sources worn or carried by the creature (such as lit torches, lanterns, or sunrods) are automatically extinguished. Once per day, the rogue can use this ability to also attempt a dispel check (as per *dispel magic*) against any magical sources of light a target carries, using her rogue level as the caster level.

Feint from Shadows (Ex): A rogue with this talent can feint in combat using a ranged weapon against a target within 30 feet and cause the opponent to lose his Dexterity modifier against her next melee or ranged attack. The rogue must have concealment (but not full concealment) from the target of the feint.

Focusing Attack* (Ex): When a rogue selects this talent, she must choose the confused, shaken, or sickened condition. When the rogue has the selected condition and hits a creature with a melee attack that deals sneak attack damage, the rogue no longer has that condition. A rogue can take this talent up to three times. Each time, she must select a different condition that she is able to remove from herself with a melee attack that deals sneak attack damage. Even if the rogue has taken this talent multiple times, she can remove only a single effect on herself with each melee attack that deals sneak attack damage.

Gloom Magic (Sp): A rogue with this talent gains the ability to cast *darkness* two times per day as a spell-like ability. The darkness created by this ability does not impair the rogue's vision. The caster level for this ability is equal to the rogue's level. A rogue must have an Intelligence score of at least 12 and the minor magic rogue talent before choosing this talent.

Greater Gloom Magic (Sp): A rogue with this talent gains the ability to cast *deeper darkness* once each day as a spell-like ability. The darkness created by this ability does not impair the rogue's vision. The caster level for this ability is equal to the rogue's level. A rogue must have an Intelligence score of at least 13 and the gloom magic and minor magic rogue talents before choosing this talent.

Mien of Despair (Su): When a rogue with this talent successfully demoralizes an opponent using the Intimidate skill or performs a successful feint against an opponent, the opponent loses any morale bonuses and cannot benefit from any morale bonuses for 1d4+1 rounds.

Obscuring Blow* (Ex): Once per day, the rogue can forgo her potential to deal sneak attack damage to attempt to cloud an opponent's vision. She must declare the use of obscuring blow before she makes the attack. If the attack hits, it does normal damage but, instead of dealing sneak attack damage (and any effect that triggers when the rogue deals sneak attack damage), the target treats all other creatures as if they had concealment, suffering a 20% miss chance on all attack rolls for a number of rounds equal to half the rogue's level.

A successful Fortitude saving throw reduces this effect to 1 round. The DC of this saving throw is equal to 10 + 1/2 the rogue's level + the rogue's Intelligence modifier.

Poison Use (Ex): The rogue is trained in the use of poison, and can't accidentally poison herself when applying poison to a weapon.

Shadow Duplicate (Sp): Once per day as an immediate action when the rogue is hit, the rogue can create a single shadow duplicate of herself, as per *mirror image*. The GM randomly determines whether the attack hit the rogue or the shadow duplicate. The shadow duplicate lasts for a number of rounds equal to the rogue's level, or until the shadow duplicate is dispelled or destroyed. This ability does not stack with the *mirror image* spell. The caster level for this ability is equal to the rogue's level. A rogue can use this ability one additional time per day for every 5 rogue levels she has.

Shadow's Chill* (Su): When a rogue with this talent hits a creature with a melee weapon that deals sneak attack damage, a number of points of the damage dealt equal to the number of sneak attack dice rolled is cold damage. The remainder of the sneak attack damage and the normal weapon damage are unaffected. The rogue must have cold resistance from a racial trait before selecting this talent.

Umbral Gear (Su): As a standard action while in an area of dim light or darkness, a rogue with this talent can coalesce wisps of shadow into a quasi-real, functional item. The rogue must choose whether to make a crowbar, 50 feet of silk rope, a glass cutter[UE], a light melee weapon with which she is proficient, a reversible cloak[UE], thieves' tools, or a wire saw[UE]; the GM may allow other similar items. The rogue can use such items for a number of minutes per day equal to 10 plus her rogue level. This duration does not need to be consecutive, but it must be used in 1-minute increments.

An item created with this ability remains until the rogue is no longer touching it, or until the rogue runs out of duration for this talent, at which time it dissolves. A rogue can select this talent more than once, gaining an additional 10 minutes of duration each time this talent is selected. If a rogue has selected this talent at least twice, she adds 50 feet of silk rope with a grappling hook, a masterwork light melee weapon with which she is proficient, and masterwork thieves' tools to the list of things she can create.

Underhanded Trick: A rogue who selects this talent gains Improved Dirty Trick[APG] as a bonus feat, even if she does not meet the prerequisites. At 6th level, she is treated as if she meets all the prerequisites for Greater Dirty Trick[APG] (although she must take the feat as normal). If she succeeds in giving her target the blinded condition, the target cannot remove the condition during the first round of blindness.

Advanced Rogue Talents

The following advanced rogue talents are available to rogues, shadowdancers, and unchained rogues[PU].

Aligned Disguise (Sp): When a rogue with this talent uses the *disguise self* spell-like ability, she can also alter her alignment aura to deceive spells that discern alignment (such as *detect evil*) for the duration of the *disguise self* effect. She can choose to detect as any specific alignment, or to detect as no alignment at all. This ability does not protect against spells or effects that cause harm based on alignment. The rogue must have *disguise self* as a spell-like ability before choosing this talent.

Blinding Strike: A rogue who selects this talent gains Blinding Critical as a bonus feat, even if she doesn't meet the prerequisites. The rogue must have the obscuring blow rogue talent and be at least 15th level before choosing this talent.

Dance of Disorienting Shadows (Ex): A rogue with this talent can attempt a Perform (dance) check in place of a combat maneuver check when attempting a reposition^{APG} combat maneuver.

Improved Shadow's Chill* (Su): When a rogue with this talent hits a creature with a melee weapon that deals sneak attack damage, the sneak attack damage is cold damage. Normal weapon damage is unaffected. The rogue must have cold resistance from a racial trait and the shadow's chill rogue talent before choosing this talent.

Reflexive Shadow Shield (Su): Once per day as an immediate action, the rogue can gain an amount of cold resistance or electricity resistance equal to half the rogue's level. This resistance lasts for 1 round. If the rogue has the shadowy resistance racial trait, the cold or electricity resistance stacks with the resistance that trait grants; otherwise, the energy resistance does not stack with any cold or electricity resistance the rogue has. The rogue must have the resiliency^{PU} rogue talent before choosing this talent.

See in Darkness (Su): The rogue gains the see in darkness ability (*Pathfinder RPG Bestiary* 2 301). A rogue must have darkvision before choosing this talent.

Shadow Walker
(Rogue Archetype)
Shadow walkers are comfortable in light, darkness, and the shadows in between. Fetchling rogues naturally gravitate toward becoming shadow walkers, but shadow walkers exist among other creatures both above and below the surface.

Expanded Sight (Su): At 1st level, a shadow walker gains darkvision with a range of 30 feet. If she already has darkvision, the range of her darkvision increases by 10 feet. When the shadow walker reaches 3rd level, and every 2 rogue levels thereafter, the range of her darkvision increases by 10 feet. Also at 3rd level, the shadow walker loses the light sensitivity weakness, if she has it. If she has light blindness, she instead treats it as light sensitivity.

This ability replaces trapfinding.

Illumination Control (Sp): At 3rd level, a shadow walker can manipulate nearby illumination. At the start of each day, a shadow walker gains a number of illumination points equal to half her rogue level and can spend illumination points to use certain spell-like abilities. As long as she has at least 1 illumination point, she can cast *light* at will. She can spend 2 illumination points to cast *darkness*, and 3 illumination points to cast *daylight*, *deeper darkness*, or *motes of dusk and dawn* (see page 28). These spell-like abilities have a caster level equal to the shadow walker's rogue level. Using these spell-like abilities does not hamper the shadow walker's vision; for example, she can see through the *deeper darkness* she creates, and does not take penalties for light sensitivity in the area of her own *daylight*.

This ability replaces the rogue talent gained at 2nd level and trap sense.

Favored Illumination (Su): At 4th level, a shadow walker chooses one illumination level: bright light, normal light, dim light, or darkness (including supernatural darkness). While she is within her chosen illumination level, she gains a +2 bonus on initiative checks and Acrobatics, Perception, and Sleight of Hand skill checks, and can take 10 on any Stealth check attempted within that illumination level. When the shadow walker confirms a critical hit with a melee attack that deals sneak attack damage while in her chosen illumination level, she regains 1 illumination point (to a maximum of half her rogue level). Confirming a critical hit on a creature that has fewer Hit Dice than half the shadow walker's character level doesn't restore illumination points. When the shadow walker reaches 6th level, and every 3 rogue levels thereafter, the bonuses she gains within her chosen illumination level increase by 1.

This ability replaces the rogue's uncanny dodge and improved uncanny dodge.

Rogue Talents: The following rogue talents complement the shadow walker archetype: deft palm^{UC}, gloom magic, greater gloom magic, obscuring blow, surprise attack, umbral gear.

Advanced Talents: The following advanced rogue talents complement the shadow walker archetype: hide in plain sight^{UC}, see in darkness, slippery mind, unwitting ally^{UC}, and weapon snatcher^{UC}.

Transformed by Light

Wayang history has been stained with forlorn sorrow since the end of the Age of Darkness, when the sun's return dissolved the interplanar corridors their kind used to trespass on Golarion from the Shadow Plane. Now trapped on the Material Plane, mostly in Tian Xia, wayangs toil on Golarion by night, only to scurry away to hidden villages when the sun rises. Despite centuries of existence in their new home, wayangs still think of themselves as creatures of shadow, and some are still able to hear the faint whispers of shadowy patrons present in their original home. Generations of being trapped on a world of inhospitable brightness has left most wayangs with dour attitudes toward life, culminating with a philosophy known as "The Dissolution," assuring wayangs that, upon their passing, their souls will finally escape the Material Plane by forever dissolving into the Shadow Plane. But while many wayangs are content to endure until the day they join their ancestors in endless night, others are drawn to leave their communes in exploration of the bright unknown, perhaps following the same otherworldly call that brought the first wayangs to Golarion millennia ago.

Wayang Alternate Racial Traits

The following racial traits can be selected instead of existing wayang racial traits.

Scion of Shadows: Some wayangs retain an uncommonly powerful connection to the Plane of Shadow. A wayang with this racial trait counts as an outsider (native) and a humanoid (wayang) for any effect related to race, including feat prerequisites and spells that affect humanoids. In addition, attacks made against such a wayang in dim light have a 50% miss chance instead of the normal 20% miss chance. This ability doesn't grant total concealment; it only increases the miss chance. This racial trait replaces light and dark and shadow resistance.

Shadow Inheritor (Su): Wayangs with exceptional ties to their shadowy heritage have great skill at manipulating shadows. A wayang with this trait treats his caster level as being 1 higher for all level-based calculations of illusion spells he casts with the darkness or shadow^UM descriptor, powers of the Darkness domain, bloodline powers of the shadow^APG bloodline, and revelations of the oracle's shadow mystery (see page 12). This trait doesn't give wayangs early access to level-based powers; it affects their effective level only for powers they could already use without this trait. This racial trait replaces shadow magic.

Shadow Speaker (Su): Countless whispers of powerful beings from the Shadow Plane—long since dead or deeply dreaming—echo in the minds of wayangs with strong spiritual connections to the darkness. These faint voices hint at revelations of things to come and suggest actions for receptive listeners to undertake. Three times per day as a free action, but no more than once per turn, a wayang with this racial trait can heed these uncanny whispers to gain a +2 insight bonus on an ability check, attack roll, caster level check, concentration check, saving throw, or skill check. The wayang must choose to use this ability before making the appropriate die roll. This racial trait replaces shadow magic.

Wayang Favored Class Options

The following options are available to all wayangs who have the listed favored class, and, unless otherwise stated, the bonus applies each time you select the favored class reward.

Barbarian: Add a +1/4 bonus to weapon damage rolls that the barbarian makes against opponents that are within dim light or darkness.

Cleric: Add a +1/2 bonus to damage rolls the cleric makes when using channel energy and casting spells that deal negative energy damage or positive energy damage, including cure and inflict spells. This bonus does not apply to healing via negative energy effects or positive energy effects.

Druid: Select one domain power granted at 1st level that is normally usable a number of times per day equal to 3 + the druid's Wisdom modifier. The druid adds +1/2 to the number of uses per day of that domain power. In addition, a druid that selects this bonus at 1st level can choose the Darkness domain with her natural bond ability.

Fighter: Add a +1/4 bonus on Stealth checks and on weapon damage rolls against flat-footed opponents.

Kineticist: Add 1/4 to the save DC of the kineticist's void infusions and wild talents (*Pathfinder Player Companion: Occult Origins* 6).

Medium: When gaining a taboo, the medium can use spirit surge without incurring influence an additional 1/4 time per day.

Monk: Add 1/6 to the monk's AC bonus.

Paladin: Add 1/3 hit point to the paladin's channel energy and lay on hands abilities (whether using it to heal or harm).

Ranger: Gain 1/6 of an additional favored terrain. Gaining a favored terrain in this manner does not increase the bonuses provided by his other favored terrains.

Rogue: The rogue gains 1/6 of a new rogue talent.

Shaman: Add one spell from the sorcerer/wizard spell list that isn't on the shaman spell list to the list of spells the shaman knows. This spell must be at least 1 level below the highest spell level the shaman can cast and be of the illusion (shadow) subschool or have the darkness descriptor.

Slayer: Add 1/4 to the studied target bonus on Bluff and Perception checks. When the slayer gains the stalker class feature, he also adds this amount to the studied target bonus on Stealth checks.

Spiritualist: Add 1/4 to the number of rounds that the spiritualist's incorporeal phantom can be out of sight and line of effect before being sent back to the Ethereal Plane.

Witch: Add one spell from the sorcerer/wizard spell list that isn't on the witch spell list to the list of spells the witch knows. This spell must be at least 1 level below the highest spell level the witch can cast and be of the illusion (shadow) subschool or have the darkness descriptor.

Wizard: Add one spell from the wizard spell list to the wizard's spellbook. The spell must be an illusion spell of the shadow subschool or have the darkness descriptor.

Wayang Feats

As trespassers upon the Material Plane, wayangs possess a variety of strange traits and features that are absent from Golarion's other inhabitants. The following feats represent wayang command over shadows and darkness, and can be taken by any wayang character that meets the prerequisites.

Extra Light and Dark

You can twist the effects of positive and negative energy for longer periods of time.

Prerequisite: Light and dark racial trait, wayang.

Benefit: Your light and dark ability lasts 1 additional minute per day.

Special: You can take this feat multiple times. Its effects stack.

Wayang Soothsayer

You embody the ideals of wayang society and culture.

Prerequisite: Wayang.

Benefit: You gain the shadow speaker racial trait (see page 10). If you already have the shadow speaker racial trait, you can increase the number of times per day that you can use shadow speaker by 1, and increase the insight bonus granted from each type of use by 1.

Special: This feat can be taken once at 1st level, and again at 11th level.

Wayang Spells

Wayangs have access to the following spell. Because it draws on the wayangs' unique physiology, spellcasters of other races cannot cast this spell.

FIRST WORLD REVISIONS

School transmutation (polymorph); **Level** alchemist 2, antipaladin 3, cleric 2, medium 2, psychic 2, sorcerer/wizard 3, witch 2
Target willing wayang touched
This spell functions as *ancestral regression*^ARG, except as noted above and as follows. The wayang loses her darkvision racial trait and gains the low-light vision racial trait in its place. The alignment and personality of the wayang are not affected by the transformation, but the spell conceals her alignment as per *undetectable alignment*. Unlike *ancestral regression*, this spell grants the target a +20 bonus on Disguise checks to pass as a gnome; even though the wayang appears as a gnomish analog of herself, the differences between gnomes and wayangs are great enough that she cannot be mistaken for a gnome by other wayangs who know her.

Other Character Options

The following options were pioneered by wayang oracles and summoners, but thousand of years of adapting them to the inhospitable brightness has enabled characters of any race to select them.

Shadow Eidolon (Unchained Summoner)

Shadow is a new eidolon subtype available to the variant of the summoner class presented in *Pathfinder RPG Pathfinder Unchained*. Summoned from the dreary shadowscapes of the Shadow Plane, shadow eidolons are grim, colorless mockeries of creatures that inhabit the Material Plane. Shadow eidolons resent being pulled into the unbearable brightness of the Material Plane. Despite this, shadow eidolons serve their summoners with somberness, acknowledging that shadow cannot exist without light.

Alignment: Any nongood.

Base Form: Biped (claws, limbs [arms], limbs [legs]), quadruped (limbs [legs, 2], bite), or serpentine (bite, improved natural armor, reach [bite], tail, tail slap).

Base Evolutions: At 1st level, shadow eidolons gain the resistance (cold) and resistance (electricity) evolutions. They also gain the ability to cast *darkness* as a spell-like ability three times per day. The caster level for this spell-like ability is equal to the eidolon's Hit Dice.

At 4th level, shadow eidolons effortlessly blend into the shadows, giving them concealment (20% miss chance) in any illumination other than bright light. In dim light or darkness, shadow eidolons have a 50% miss chance instead of the normal 20% miss chance; this doesn't grant the eidolons total concealment. A shadow eidolon can suspend or resume this ability as a free action.

At 8th level, shadow eidolons gain DR 5/magic and increase the range of their darkvision to 90 feet. In addition, they add 1 point to their evolution pools.

At 12th level, shadow eidolons lose the ability to cast *darkness* as a spell-like ability and instead gain the ability to cast *deeper darkness* as a spell-like ability three times per day. In addition, they gain the see in darkness universal monster ability.

At 16th level, shadow eidolons' damage reduction increases to DR 10/magic and they gain the spell resistance evolution.

At 20th level, shadow eidolons increase the range of their darkvision to 120 feet and gain the ability to cast *shadow step* as a spell-like ability at will. Three times per day, a shadow eidolon can quicken this spell-like ability, functioning as the Quicken Spell-Like Ability feat.

Shadow Ink Tattoos

Wayangs are known for ritualistically scarring themselves, and this form of artistic expression has led to the widespread use of the following magical tattoos across Tian Xia and beyond.

MESMERIZING TATTOO		PRICE 10,800 GP
SLOT none	CL 5th	WEIGHT —
AURA faint enchantment		

This shadowy tattoo is drawn in a spiraling pattern down one of the bearer's arms. If the tattoo is visible, the wearer gains a +2 circumstance bonus on Diplomacy checks.

Whenever the bearer uses the hypnotism occult skill unlock[OA], casts an enchantment spell that targets a single creature, or uses the hypnotic stare[OA] class feature, her target takes a –1 penalty on Will saving throws for the ability's duration and the DC to affect the target with the hypnotism occult skill unlock is reduced by 1. This is a mind-affecting effect.

CONSTRUCTION REQUIREMENTS	COST 5,400 GP

Inscribe Magical Tattoo (*Pathfinder Campaign Setting: Inner Sea Magic* 16), *suggestion*

PENUMBRA TATTOO		PRICE 24,000 GP
SLOT none	CL 3rd	WEIGHT —
AURA faint evocation		

This ritualistic scar is infused with shadowstuff that shifts and writhes within the bearer's skin. Whenever the bearer is exposed to illumination brighter than dim light, the tattoo emits a vapor, shrouding the bearer in a dusky haze that provides the benefits of *protective penumbra*[UM].

CONSTRUCTION REQUIREMENTS	COST 12,000 GP

Inscribe Magical Tattoo (*Inner Sea Magic* 16), *protective penumbra*[UM]

SWIRLING SMOKE TATTOO		PRICE 12,500 GP
SLOT none	CL 5th	WEIGHT —
AURA faint enchantment		

This simple tattoo emits a constant haze of odorless, shadowy smoke around the limbs of its bearer that she can animate with a thought, hiding herself behind a screen of smoke. If the tattoo is visible when the bearer is hit by a melee or ranged attack or when the bearer fails a Reflex save, the wearer can activate the tattoo to shroud herself in mist as an immediate action. This imposes a 20% miss chance on attacks made against the bearer. On a failed Reflex save, it grants the ability to reroll the Reflex save and gain a +4 bonus. The bearer can use this ability three times per day.

CONSTRUCTION REQUIREMENTS	COST 6,250 GP

Inscribe Magical Tattoo (*Inner Sea Magic* 16), *blur*

Shadow (Oracle Mystery)

Deities: Groetus, Lao Shu Po, Tsukiyo, Zon-Kuthon.

Class Skills: An oracle with this mystery adds Bluff, Disguise, Knowledge (dungeoneering), and Stealth to her list of class skills.

Bonus Spells: *Blurred movement*[ACG] (2nd), *invisibility* (4th), *deeper darkness* (6th), *shadow step*[UM] (8th), *vampiric shadow shield*[ACG] (10th), *shadow walk* (12th), *mass invisibility* (14th), *greater shadow evocation* (16th), *shades* (18th).

Revelations: An oracle with the shadow mystery can choose from any of the following revelations.

Army of Darkness (Su): Whenever you cast a *summon monster* spell and summon a creature that normally has the celestial or fiendish template, you can instead summon it with the shadow creature template (*Pathfinder RPG Bestiary 4* 238). This revelation counts as having the Spell Focus (conjuration) feat for the purpose of meeting the prerequisites of the Augment Summoning feat, as well as any feat that lists Augment Summoning as a prerequisite.

Cloak of Darkness (Su): This ability functions as the dark tapestry mystery[UM] revelation of the same name.

Dark Secrets (Su): You learn the hidden secrets surrounding the casting of shadow spells. You can add a number of spells from the sorcerer/wizard spell list equal to your Charisma modifier (minimum 1, maximum equal to half your oracle level) to your spell list and your list of spells known as divine spells. These have a spell level equal to their sorcerer/wizard spell level. You can add only illusion spells from the shadow subschool or spells with the darkness descriptor to your list of spells known in this manner. Each time you gain an oracle level after taking this revelation, you can choose to replace one of these spells for a new appropriate spell on the sorcerer/wizard spell list.

Living Shadow (Sp): Your body dissolves, and you become a living shadow. This ability functions as *gaseous form*. At 14th level, this ability functions as *shadow body*^{OA} instead, except you also gain DR 10/magic and become immune to poison, sneak attacks, and critical hits as if also using *gaseous form*. You can use this ability a number of minutes per day equal to your oracle level. This duration does not need to be consecutive, but it must be spent in 1-minute increments. You must be at least 7th level to choose this revelation.

Pierce the Shadows (Su): The shadows step aside from your baleful gaze, affording you sight in even the deepest darkness. You gain darkvision 60 feet. If you already have darkvision, increase your existing darkvision by 60 feet instead. At 11th level, you can see perfectly in darkness of any kind, even in absolute darkness or the darkness created by a *deeper darkness* spell.

Shadow Armament (Su): You can create a quasi-real simple or martial masterwork weapon appropriate for your current size. You are considered proficient with this weapon. The first time you hit a creature with this weapon, that creature can attempt a Will save to disbelieve; failure means the weapon deals damage normally, while success means the creature takes only 1 point of damage from the weapon's attacks. The weapon deals only 1 point of damage to objects. At 3rd level, and again at 11th level and 19th level, the weapon gains a cumulative +1 enhancement bonus. At 7th level, the weapon gains either the *frost* or *keen* weapon special ability, chosen when the weapon is created. These abilities don't function against a target that succeeds at its Will save. At 15th level, the weapon deals minimum damage (as if it had rolled a 1 on each of its damage dice) against targets that succeed at their saves instead of 1 point of damage. You can use this ability for a number of minutes per day equal to your oracle level. This duration does not need to be consecutive, but it must be used in 1-minute increments. The weapon disappears after 1 round if it leaves your grasp.

Shadow Mastery (Su): Whenever you cast an illusion spell from the shadow subschool, increase the strength of such spells by 1% per oracle level you have. You must be at least 7th level to choose this revelation.

Shadow Projection (Su): You infuse your life force and psyche into your shadow, causing it to separate from your body and act as an independent creature. This ability functions as *shadow projection*^{APG} except as follows. Your shadow has the outsider type and the phantom subtype instead of the undead type. As a result, this ability does not have the evil descriptor and your shadow cannot be turned or affected as undead (though it can be affected as an outsider). You can use this ability for a number of hours per day equal to half your oracle level. These hours don't need to be consecutive, but they must be spent in 1-hour increments. Your shadow's hit points are not replenished between uses, although your shadow can be healed in the same manner as any other outsider. When this ability isn't in use, any healing done to you also heals your shadow for an equal amount. You must be at least 7th level to choose this revelation.

Stealth Mastery (Ex): You gain Skill Focus with the Stealth skill. At 8th level, you gain Signature Skill^{PU} with the

Stealth skill, even if you don't meet the feat's prerequisites. At 16th level, you gain the hide in plain sight shadowdancer class feature.

Wings of Darkness (Su): This ability functions as the dark tapestry mystery^{UM} revelation of the same name. You must be at least 7th level to select this revelation.

Final Revelation: Upon reaching 20th level, your body becomes permanently suffused with the essence of the Shadow Plane. You gain regeneration 5 while in dim light or darkness and immunity to cold, critical hits, and sneak attacks. Your regeneration is suppressed while in any level of illumination brighter than dim light. In addition, any spells you cast of the shadow subschool or with the darkness descriptor are automatically enlarged without affecting their spell level.

Transformed by the Darklands

For millennia, the drow have reigned as one of the most powerful races of the Darklands. As the ancient elves fled the destruction of Earthfall, the inhospitable darkness of their new subterranean home left them vulnerable to divine and demonic influences. Over time, the surviving elves adapted to their lightless refuge, bodies and souls warped by powerful magic as they embraced barbarism and slavery. Deep below the sunlit world, vast cities like Zirnakaynin now occupy immense caverns in Sekamina, the middle layer of the Darklands. Today, a dark elf that ascends to the surface of Golarion hails from a culture that sacrificed its elven heritage on the brutal, bloody altar of survival.

The drow divide "surface seekers" into two categories. Rejects flee the Darklands in search of an easier life. Unable to stomach the hard truths of survival among a master race, they abandon their families to find peace and shelter. Only marginally more respected are the upstarts, who see opportunity in the soft underbellies of surface civilizations. To upstart drow, humans and other common races weigh themselves down with laws and moral structures, expanding the gap in power between themselves and the drow who take advantage of their vulnerabilities.

Drow or Half-Elf Alternate Racial Traits

There is perhaps no lonelier creature than a half-elf with a drow parent. Viewed as an insult to family by the drow and as alien and villainous to humans, half-drow are as likely as any to flee their homes and traverse the Darklands (in either direction) in search of a place to call home. The majority of these are regarded by drow as upstarts—runts lacking the natural superiority of their purebred siblings. Unfortunately, half-drow find little solace under the sun, frequently greeted as precursors to slave raids or pitied as if their elven heritages were a disease.

Drow or half-elves can select from among the following racial traits instead of existing drow or half-elf racial traits, either to represent drow with non-drow influences in their physiology or half-elves with drow lineages.

Daylight Adaptation: Some drow with a hint of other racial heritages spend significant time on the surface and maintain their darkvision, but no longer have the light blindness trait. This racial trait replaces spell resistance.

Drow Heritage: Half-elves with this trait count as drow for the purposes of any effect related to race, including prerequisites. This racial trait replaces the ability to choose any language as a bonus language, instead limiting the character to the bonus languages offered to drow.

Flexible Half-Breed: Once per day, half-elves with this trait can use *alter self* as a spell-like ability to appear as humans, drow, or elves. The half-elf can change the race of this form each time she uses this ability, but the specific form for each race is static. She gains a +10 bonus to Disguise checks to appear as a member of the chosen race. The caster level for this ability is equal to the character's Hit Dice. This racial trait replaces multitalented.

Hidden Half-Breed: In benign communities, half-elves endure assumptions and bigotry based on ignorance and suspicion. In drow society, public knowledge of one's mixed ancestry can mean a cruel death. Half-elves with this trait gain a +2 bonus on Bluff and Disguise checks to pass as full-blooded drow, elves, or humans. This racial trait replaces the ability to choose any language as a bonus language, instead limiting the character to the bonus languages offered to drow.

Lesser Spell-Like Abilities: Half-elves with this trait can cast *dancing lights*, *darkness*, and *faerie fire* once each per day.

The caster level for these effects is equal to the user's character level. This racial trait replaces adaptability and multitalented.

Psychic Sensitivity: The Darklands is full of strange energies, and the drow or half-drow who live there practice bloody rituals in exchange for favor and power. Drow or half-elves with this trait gain the Psychic Sensitivity feat (*Pathfinder Roleplaying Game Occult Adventures* 138), gaining access to occult skill unlocks normally only available to psychic spellcasters. This racial trait replaces keen senses for drow and half-elves and drow immunities for drow or elven immunities for half-elves.

Shade Magic: Drow with this trait can cast *cloak of shade*^APG, *dust of twilight*^APG, and *ghost sound* as spell-like abilities each once per day. This racial trait replaces a drow's normal spell-like abilities.

Shadow Sorcery: Drow with this trait have a supernatural affinity for shadow. A drow sorcerer with the shadow^APG bloodline treats her Charisma score as 2 points higher for all sorcerer class abilities and for spells with the shadow^UM descriptor she casts. This racial trait replaces poison use.

Spell Resistance: Some drow-blooded half-elves share the drow resistance to magic. A half-elf with this racial trait gains spell resistance equal to 6 + her character level. This racial trait replaces adaptability and keen senses.

Drow Favored Class Options

With omnipresent peril and a long list of talents, drow pursue a wide variety of adventuring occupations both above- and belowground. The rules below allow drow to take alternate rewards when they gain a level in one of the following classes.

Bard: Add +1/2 to Bluff and Disguise checks to appear as an elf or half-elf.

Bloodrager: Add a +1/2 bonus to concentration checks to cast or maintain spells when taking damage.

Druid: Add a +1 bonus to wild empathy checks to influence animals and magical beasts that live underground.

Inquisitor: Gain 1/4 of a teamwork feat.

Paladin: Add a +1/2 sacred bonus to saving throws against spells of the shadow subschool or that have the darkness or shadow^UM descriptor.

Psychic: Gain 1/6 of a phrenic amplification (or a major amplification if the psychic is at least 11th level).

Ranger: Add +1/3 to initiative checks in one of the ranger's favored terrains.

Summoner: Add 1 hit point or 1 skill rank to the summoner's eidolon.

Warpriest: Add 1/2 point to the amount of damage dealt or healed by the warpriest's fervor ability.

Drow or Half-Elf Feats

The following drow and half-elf feats remain most common in drow societies.

Drow Spirit

Although you are of mixed heritage, the magic of your drow relatives flows freely through your veins.

Prerequisite: Half-elf.

Benefit: You gain the ability to cast *dancing lights*, *darkness*, and *faerie fire* each once per day as a spell-like ability. You use your character level as your caster level for these abilities. Alternatively, you can instead gain any one racial trait that elves can exchange for the elven magic racial trait.

Special: You can take this feat only at 1st level. If you take this feat, you cannot take the Human Spirit^ARG or Elven Spirit^ARG feat.

Surface Scout

You were trained from youth to infiltrate and ambush aboveground settlements.

Prerequisites: Drow, spell-like abilities drow racial trait.

Benefit: You can use *fear the sun* and *ignoble form* (see below) each once per day as a spell-like ability. Your caster level is equal to your character level.

Drow Spells

Drow magic relies on shadow and stealth, but also employs necromantic and transformational magic. The following spells were developed by drow, but have since made their way into spellbooks across the surface world.

DARKVAULT

School abjuration; **Level** alchemist 3, cleric 5, druid 5, psychic 5, shaman 5, sorcerer/wizard 5, witch 5

Casting Time 1 standard action

Components V, S, M (a stone that has never seen sunlight)

Range close (25 ft. + 5 ft./2 levels)

Area 30-ft.-radius emanation

Duration 24 hours

Saving Throw none; **Spell Resistance** no

You ward an area's shadows such that light cannot penetrate them. The illumination level in the affected area no longer changes when nonmagical light enters it. Any magical effect must succeed at a caster level check (DC = 10 + your caster level) in order to change the light level within the spell's radius. *Darkvault* has no effect on spells or effects that would make the spell's area darker.

The spell must be cast on an area, such as a cave or room. A spellcaster of 11th level or higher can make *darkvault* permanent with a *permanency* spell, at a cost of 7,500 gp.

FEAR THE SUN

School transmutation; **Level** antipaladin 1, bloodrager 1, cleric 2, druid 2, inquisitor 2, occultist 2, psychic 2, shaman 2, sorcerer/wizard 2, witch 2

Casting Time 1 standard action

Components V, S, M (a drow eyelash)

Range medium (100 ft. + 10 ft./level)

Target up to one creature/level, no two of which can be more than 30 ft. apart

Duration 1 round/level

Saving Throw Fortitude negates; **Spell Resistance** yes

Each target that fails its saving throw gains light blindness, as per the universal monster rule. When exposed to bright light, affected targets are blinded for 1 full round and are dazzled in successive rounds. If you cast this spell in the presence of bright light, any target that fails its save is blinded immediately, and dazzled starting at the beginning of its first turn.

IGNOBLE FORM

School transmutation (polymorph); **Level** alchemist 2, antipaladin 2, bard 2, druid 3, medium 2, ranger 2, sorcerer/wizard 4, witch 4

Casting Time 1 standard action

Components V, S, M (a half-elf ear)

Range touch

Target one drow

Duration 24 hours

Saving Throw Fortitude negates (harmless); **Spell Resistance** no

The target takes on the form of a half-elf from the surface world. Its skin, hair, and eyes change to match a specific human ethnicity. You can even change the target's facial features or produce light facial hair or stubble. The target loses its darkvision, light blindness, and light sensitivity traits, if it normally has them. The target gains low-light vision; a +3 racial bonus on a single Craft, Knowledge, Perform, or Profession skill of its choice; and both a +4 bonus on Bluff checks and a +10 bonus on Disguise checks to pass itself off as a half-elf.

SHADOWMIND

School illusion [phantasm]; **Level** antipaladin 2, cleric 3, druid 3, inquisitor 2, mesmerist 3, occultist 3, psychic 3, shaman 3, sorcerer/wizard 3, witch 2

Casting Time 1 standard action

Components V, S, M (a small square of black silk)

Range medium (100 ft. + 10 ft./level)

Target up to one creature/level, no two of which can be more than 30 ft. apart

Duration 1 minute/level

Saving Throw Will negates; **Spell Resistance** yes

You dim your targets' perceptions of light and shadow, convincing them the space they occupy is dark. Each creature that fails its save perceives the world around it as one light level darker than its true illumination level. The spell does not change the light level outside of the targets' perception, and does not create magical darkness. However, the spell creates an illusion of darkness rather than actual darkness, so low-light and darkvision don't allow a target to see in the conditions created by the spell. Even targets that see normally through magical darkness suffer a loss of vision from this spell.

UMBRAL STRIKE

School necromancy (shadow) [darkness]; **Level** cleric 7, druid 7, inquisitor 6, magus 6, occultist 6, psychic 7, shaman 7, sorcerer/wizard 7, spiritualist 6, witch 7

Casting Time 1 standard action

Components V, S, M (a black crossbow bolt)

Range medium (100 ft. + 10 ft./level)

Target 1 creature

Duration 1 round/level

Saving Throw Fortitude partial; **Spell Resistance** yes

You create a bolt of dark energy and use it to make a ranged touch attack that ignores concealment (but not total concealment).

If you hit, the target takes 1d6 points of damage per caster level (maximum 20d6). Half of this damage is cold damage and half of it is negative energy. The bolt's shadow expands and covers the target, rendering him blind for the duration of the spell. A successful Fortitude save halves the damage and negates the blind condition.

Other Class Options

Drow societies exist in realms of endless gloom, making the power of darkness an obvious choice for exploration. Though the following class options are most common among the drow, any creature adopted by or born into shadow can choose them.

Shadow (Bloodrager Bloodline)

Because of your heritage, you can move and see through shadows as if you are part of them. Your fury absorbs light, warmth, and strength.

Bonus Feats: Blind-Fight, Combat Reflexes, Improved Initiative, Lightning Reflexes, Quick Draw, Step Up.

Bonus Spells: *Ray of enfeeblement* (7th), *darkvision* (10th), *deeper darkness* (13th), *shadow conjuration* (16th).

Bloodline Powers: Your bloodline gives you powers over light and darkness.

Shadow Vision (Su): While bloodraging, you gain low-light vision if you don't already have it. If you already have low-light vision, you gain darkvision to a distance of 30 feet. At 10th level, you gain darkvision with a range of 30 feet, or add 30 feet to the range of your darkvision if you already have it.

Shades of Rage (Su): At 4th level, whenever you enter a bloodrage, the light level within 30 feet of you decreases by one step. Natural light is always affected, but magical illumination dispels this ability if the caster of the light effect succeeds at a caster level check against a DC equal to 10 + your class level.

Strength of Shadows (Su): At 8th level, you gain cold resistance 10. Your melee attacks deal additional cold damage equal to the critical multiplier of the weapon you use. At 13th level, your cold resistance increases to 20. At 18th level, you become immune to cold damage.

Strike Through Shadow (Su): At 12th level, you can declare a single melee attack as a strike through shadow. This attack moves through its target's shadow and strikes from below or inside its armor. You make this attack against the target's touch AC. You can use this ability once per day, plus an additional time per day each at 15th and 18th levels.

Shadow Door (Su): At 16th level, you can take any part of your movement through shadows, teleporting to another location within 60 feet. This ability functions as *dimension door*, except you can't use shadow door in brightly lit areas. You can teleport in this manner a total of 10 feet per class level each day.

Shadow Warrior (Su): At 20th level, you become shadow and fury personified. You see perfectly in natural and magical darkness. Whenever you deal hit point damage with a spell or attack, you also deal 2 points of Strength damage to each creature that took damage.

Shadow Subdomain (Cleric Subdomain)

Associated Domains: Darkness, Death.

Deities: Nocticula, Norgorber, Urgathoa, Zon-Kuthon.

Granted Powers: The following granted power replaces the touch of darkness ability of the Darkness domain or the bleeding touch ability of the Death domain.

Whispering Shadows (Su): You can darken the shadows around you and cause them to hiss, confounding and distracting your enemies. As an immediate action, you can force a target within 30 feet to reroll a miss chance due to concealment or a saving throw against an illusion or necromancy spell. The target of this ability must keep the result of the second roll, even if it is worse than the original roll. You can use this ability a number of times per day equal to 3 + your Wisdom modifier.

Replacement Domain Spells: 1st—*ray of enfeeblement*, 4th—*phantasmal killer*, 8th—*orb of the void*[UM]

Shadow (Psychic Discipline)

You perceive the space between light and darkness, and draw power from it. Shadows conceal and protect you, while revealing the locations of those who dare to hide within them. Over time, you develop the ability to deny the warmth of light or life to your enemies.

Phrenic Pool Ability: Wisdom.

Bonus Spells: *blurred movement*[ACG] (2nd), *fear the sun* (4th), *deeper darkness* (6th), *shadow step*[UM] (8th), *shadow evocation* (10th), *shadow walk* (12th), *lunar veil*[UM] (14th), *umbral strike* (16th), *polar midnight*[UM] (18th).

Discipline Powers: Your powers give you authority over light and shadow.

Twilight Influence (Su): You can channel spell energy into spells drawn from the Darkness cleric domain. This ability functions similarly to the cleric's ability to spontaneously cast cure or inflict spells, but you instead spontaneously cast Darkness domain spells. The domain spells don't count as being on your psychic spell list for the purposes of any other effects (unless they are independently on your psychic spell list, such as *blindness/deafness*). Each day, you can convert up to one spell from each spell level you can cast. Each time you use this ability to convert a spell, you regain 1 point in your phrenic pool. The maximum number of points you can regain in this way per day is equal to your Wisdom modifier.

Dark Defense (Su): At 5th level, light and darkness become your allies, moving around you to protect you from your enemies. You gain a +2 deflection bonus to Armor Class against any attack while you benefit from concealment against that attack. If you have full concealment from that attack, this deflection bonus increases to +4.

Adumbration (Su): At 13th level, shadows move to conceal you. You gain a bonus on Stealth checks equal to half your level. In addition, you can use the Stealth skill even while being observed and without cover or concealment, as long as you are within 10 feet of a shadow other than your own. You gain no benefit from adumbration in areas of bright light.

Shadow Blessing (Warpriest Blessing)

Deities: Nocticula, Norgorber, Zon-Kuthon.

Flicker of Shadows (minor): At 1st level, you can cause a weapon you touch to warp and become insubstantial for a split second before an attack. The first attack made with this weapon each round ignores any shield bonus to Armor Class, as well as bonuses from cover. Total cover still provides a creature its full benefit. This effect lasts for 1 minute.

Swift as Shadow (major): At 10th level, you can spend a swift action to empower yourself or an ally within 30 feet to move over the ground as easily as its shadow. The subject's land speed increases by 10 feet and it takes no movement penalties for darkness, difficult terrain, or slickness. The creature can safely move over areas of ice and even those affected by a *grease* spell. When a creature affected by this ability hits with a charge attack, that attack deals an amount of additional cold damage equal to your level.

Shadowy Archetypes

Many heroes delve into dark locales, which might be to their detriment if they lack proper preparations. However, rather than be impeded by these environments, some adventurers embrace the shadows and add them to their arsenal. These individuals learn to fight with this powerful tool and triumph over those who try to do the same.

Dusk Knight (Paladin Archetype)

Some paladins focus their training to combat the shadows and use darkness to their advantage. Known as dusk knights, these paladins are primarily worshipers of Abadar, but dusk knights who serve Iomedae and Irori, though rare, do exist.

Skills: A dusk knight adds Stealth to her list of class skills, instead of Sense Motive.

This alters the paladin's class skills.

Shadow Smite (Su): A dusk knight gains concealment for 1 round per paladin level against the target of her smite evil ability in addition to its other effects. The dusk knight doesn't deal additional damage with her smite evil ability.

This ability alters smite evil.

Illuminating Zeal (Su): At 4th level, a dusk knight gains the ability to grant darkvision to her allies. As a standard action, the dusk knight grants one target touched darkvision with a range of 60 feet for 1 hour. If the target already has darkvision, the range increases by 60 feet instead. If the dusk knight targets herself, using this ability is a swift action. Using this ability consumes two uses of her lay on hands ability.

This ability replaces channel positive energy.

Shadow's Embrace (Su): At 5th level, a dusk knight learns to fight effectively in areas of darkness. She gains Blind-Fight as a bonus feat and darkvision with a range of 60 feet. If she already has darkvision, the range increases by 30 feet instead. At 10th level, a dusk knight gains Improved Blind-Fight as a bonus feat. At 15th level, a dusk knight gains the see in darkness ability.

This ability replaces divine bond.

Cloak of Shadow (Su): At 8th level, a dusk knight becomes adept at moving through darkness. She ignores her armor penalty when attempting Stealth checks and gains a bonus on Stealth checks equal to half her paladin level while in areas of dim light or darkness.

This ability replaces aura of resolve.

Clouding Smite (Su): At 11th level, a dusk knight's smite impairs her foe's abilities in the dark. When a dusk knight successfully smites a foe, she reduces the target's darkvision by 60 feet for the duration of the smite. If the target has the see in darkness ability, it must succeed at a Fortitude save or lose this ability for the duration of the smite. The save DC is equal to 10 + 1/2 the dusk knight's paladin level + her Charisma modifier.

This ability replaces aura of justice.

Gloom Chymist (Alchemist Archetype)

A breakthrough in Nidalese alchemy led to the creation of glooms, magical fields of darkness from the Shadow Plane that can be momentarily animated with the use of strange compounds. These mixtures are quite efficacious, leading to the spread of their use throughout the rest of the Inner Sea region.

Gloom (Su): A gloom chymist is skilled at mixing potent concoctions known as glooms, which are infused with shadow energy. A gloom is identical to a bomb except that it deals 1d6 points of cold damage + additional damage equal to the gloom chymist's Intelligence modifier. This damage increases by 1d6 for every 2 alchemist levels beyond 1st the gloom chymist has. A gloom does not qualify as a bomb for the purposes of feats or discoveries.

This ability replaces bomb.

Umbral Gloom (Su): At 2nd level, whenever a gloom chymist makes a gloom, he can have it increase or decrease the light level by one step within its splash radius, in addition to its other effects. This change lasts for a number of rounds equal to the gloom chymist's Intelligence modifier. At 8th level, the gloom chymist expend two uses of his daily glooms to increase or decrease light levels as per *daylight* or *deeper darkness*, respectively, using his alchemist level as the caster level.

This ability replaces poison resistance, poison use, and swift poisoning.

Discoveries

The following new discoveries can be taken by any alchemist who meets the prerequisites and has the gloom class feature. Discoveries that modify glooms are marked with a single asterisk (*) and do not stack. Only one such discovery can be applied to an individual gloom.

Bounding Gloom: The alchemist gains the ability to travel between shadows as if by means of a *dimension door* spell. The limitation is that the alchemist's beginning and ending locations must be areas of dim light or darker, or within the radius of an umbral gloom that is lowering the light level. The alchemist can travel up to a total of 100 feet each day in this way. This distance must be used in 10-foot increments; for example, the alchemist can make a single jump of 100 feet or 10 jumps of 10 feet each. For every 2 levels beyond 10th, the distance the alchemist can jump each day doubles (200 feet at 12th level, 400 feet at 14th level, and so on). An alchemist must be at least 10th level before selecting this discovery.

Debilitating Gloom*: A creature struck by the gloom must make a successful Fortitude save or take a penalty to its Strength equal to 1d4 + 1 per 2 alchemist levels (maximum of 1d4+5) for 1 round per alchemist level. A target's Strength score cannot drop below 1. This penalty does not stack with itself. An alchemist must be at least 6th level before selecting this discovery.

Draining Gloom*: A creature struck by a direct hit with the gloom must make a successful Fortitude save or gain 1 negative level. An alchemist must be at least 8th level and must have the debilitating gloom discovery before selecting this discovery.

Glutinous Gloom*: The gloom creates an area in its splash radius that functions as *web*. The webbing lasts for a number of rounds equal to 1/2 the alchemist's level. An alchemist must be at least 6th level before selecting this discovery.

Grasping Gloom*: The gloom creates an area equal to double its splash radius that functions as *black tentacles*. The effect lasts for a number of rounds equal to half the alchemist's level. An alchemist must be at least 8th level before selecting this discovery.

Greater Draining Gloom*: A creature struck by the gloom must succeed at a Fortitude save or gain 1d4 negative levels. An alchemist must be at least 12th level and must have the debilitating gloom and draining gloom discoveries before selecting this discovery.

Mucilaginous Gloom*: The gloom leaves a chilly gray residue that turns each square in its splash radius into difficult terrain. This effect lasts for a number of rounds equal to the alchemist's level.

Rime-Bound Gloom*: The gloom creates an area of freezing shadow in its splash radius that deals 2d6 points of cold damage to all creatures in the area each turn. This effect lasts 1 round for every 2 alchemist levels. An alchemist must be at least 6th level to select this discovery.

Umbral Scion (Sorcerer Archetype)

Umbral scions are sorcerers who are able to expertly control their especially potent shadow heritage. The majority of umbral sorcerers hail from the Darklands.

Bloodline: An umbral scion must have the shadow[APG] bloodline.

Diminished Spellcasting: An umbral scion can cast one fewer spell per day of each level than normal. If this reduces the number to 0, she can cast spells of that level only if her Charisma score grants her bonus spells of that level.

This ability alters the sorcerer's spellcasting.

Shrouded Spells (Su): An umbral scion is enveloped by wisps of shadow whenever she casts a spell. The DC to identify spells cast by an umbral scion increases by 2. If the spell is being cast within an area of dim light or darkness, the DC increases by 5 instead.

Encroaching Darkness (Su): An umbral scion is capable of influencing light around her. As a standard action, she can produce a 10-foot-radius veil centered on a creature or object within 30 feet. This veil decreases the light level by one step and remains for a number of rounds equal to the sorcerer's Charisma modifier. At 7th level, the veil increases to a 30-foot radius. At 8th level, the veil decreases the light level by two steps. If the light level is decreased past darkness, the veil is treated as *deeper darkness*. At 14th level, the veil increases to 60 feet and grants any creature within it cover (even against senses normally able to penetrate total darkness, such as the see in darkness ability). An umbral scion can use this ability a number of times per day equal to 3 + her Charisma modifier.

This ability replaces the shadowstrike bloodline power.

Potent Shadows (Su): At 7th level, when an umbral scion casts a spell of the shadow subschool or a spell with the darkness or shadow[UM] descriptor within an area of dim light or darkness, she treats her caster level as 1 higher. Only the sorcerer herself needs to be in dim light or darkness. This bonus increases by 1 every 4 sorcerer levels beyond 7th she has to a maximum of +4 at 19th level.

This ability replaces the 7th-level bloodline feat.

Crippling Darkness (Su): At 13th level, when an umbral scion targets a creature within an area of dim light or darkness with a spell of the shadow subschool or a spell with the darkness or shadow[UM] descriptor, the DC for the spell increases by 1. This bonus increases by 1 at 18th level.

This ability replaces the 13th-level bloodline feat.

Fighting in the Dark

Every adventurer eventually finds herself in shadowy places, whether they're dark ruins or lightless caves. For most, darkness can be an unwelcome obstacle, though creatures such as dwarves and half-orcs have darkvision to pierce lightless places for a fair distance. Other races find the absence of light much more burdensome. Managing in the dark is a troublesome prospect, but the strategies offered below will help any adventurer feel more comfortable in such circumstances.

General Tactics

Developing a proper strategy for fighting in darkness requires an understanding of how light works. In brief, light is measured in levels: bright light, normal light, dim light, darkness, and, occasionally, supernatural darkness. The ambient light that exists before characters potentially start changing it determines an area's initial light level. A number of items and spells can alter this light level and combat the detriment of darkness.

The most obvious ways to cast light are torches, lanterns, and even simple candles. Alchemical sources, such as sunrods and candlerods (*Pathfinder RPG Ultimate Equipment* 102), provide similar illumination for far longer. Also, spells such as *daylight* can illuminate a naturally dark area or negate all magical darkness and return the light to an ambient level. Dispersing multiple light sources in a dark area creates areas of dim light, allowing further visibility in the dark. These areas are especially useful for creatures with low-light vision, which doubles the effective radius of each light source.

Although creatures with darkvision are at home in the dark, there are still ways to hide from them. Trees, large rocks, and short walls remain great hiding places regardless of the light level. If stealth isn't possible, concealment is always an option. Smokesticks and spells such as *fog cloud* obscure vision for all creatures, regardless of their abilities. In many cases, darkvision is limited to a range of 60 feet, allowing characters to hide from such creatures beyond that distance.

Specific Tactics

Magic items can be great tools to chase away the darkness. Specific magic weapons and armors, such as a *glorious* weapon (*Ultimate Equipment* 142) or *radiant* armor (*Ultimate Equipment* 121), can generate their own bright glows. An everburning torch or an *ioun torch* (*Ultimate Equipment* 305) offers a limitless light source, while certain magic items provide darkvision, such as *goggles of night*.

Numerous spells can ease the effort of combat in the dark. Spells such as *continual flame*, *dancing lights*, *daylight*, and *light* produce varying levels of light that might even hamper creatures with light sensitivity or light blindness. Instead of illuminating the dark, *alter self*, *beast shape*, *darkvision*, and other similar spells grant you the ability to see in the dark, allowing the caster to function without revealing his location with bright lights. Additionally, the *deeper darkness* spell prevents even creatures with basic darkvision from seeing in the dark.

Deeper darkness does not prevent the rare creature with the see in darkness supernatural ability (*Pathfinder RPG Bestiary 2* 301) from seeing. Creatures with this ability include devils and dark folk. Players who make the proper choices for their characters are able to gain this ability as well—for example, oracles with the dark tapestry mystery or rogues who take the see in darkness advanced rogue talent (see page 9). All characters can benefit from a similar ability by consuming an *elixir of darksight* (*Pathfinder RPG Advanced Race Guide* 19).

Illumination Magic Items

Light can be manipulated and used as a tool in a variety of ways, leading to the creation of many magical objects and weapons. A number of illuminating items are presented here.

BEAMING	PRICE +1 bonus
AURA faint evocation	**CL** 10th

Only ranged weapons can have the *beaming* ability. Once per day, as a swift action, a *beaming* weapon creates a number of glowing orbs equal to the weapon's enhancement bonus. The orbs float around the wielder's head like a halo and fire rays of light at the wielder's foes. Once per round when the wielder makes an attack or full-attack with the *beaming* weapon, the wielder can expend one orb as a free action to fire a beam of *searing light* at any target within range. The orbs remain until expended or until the wielder sleeps.

CONSTRUCTION REQUIREMENTS	COST +1 bonus

Craft Magic Arms and Armor, *searing light*

BRILLIANT BULWARK	PRICE 9,655 GP	
SLOT none	**CL** 10th	**WEIGHT** 4 lbs.
AURA moderate evocation		

This *+1 blinding*[UE] *buckler* is made from a lustrous glass that is as hard as steel and reflects light like a mirror. The shield glows as a torch, though this light can be suppressed or resumed on command. The shield can be commanded to shine light as per *daylight* for up to 10 minutes each day. This duration need not be consecutive, but it must be used in 1-minute increments. The wielder can also expend this duration while activating the buckler's *blinding* ability to increase the save DC by 1 for every 2 minutes of *daylight* duration expended. The shield must sit in natural bright light for at least 1 hour after its 10 minutes of *daylight* is expended before the ability can be used again.

CONSTRUCTION REQUIREMENTS	COST 4,975 GP

Craft Magic Arms and Armor, *daylight*, *light*

FAITHFUL LANTERN	PRICE 2,500 GP	
SLOT none	**CL** 9th	**WEIGHT** 2 lbs.
AURA moderate abjuration and conjuration		

This fine, silver bullseye lantern is embossed with the image of a stoic sentinel. It functions as a bullseye lantern that doesn't require oil to function. On command, the lantern floats alongside its user, shedding its light in whichever direction the user is looking.

Once per day on command, the lantern can be designated to stand guard for up to 8 hours. The lantern ceases to shed light and keeps watch over a 30-foot-radius area centered on itself. The lantern acts as the *alarm* spell, except it is activated only by creatures that are Small or larger, and it cannot see invisible creatures. If the lantern detects a creature, it notifies the user that commanded the lantern with a mental alarm, waking the user if necessary. Once the lantern notifies its user, it shines its light on the intruder until commanded to stop.

CONSTRUCTION REQUIREMENTS	COST 1,250 GP

Craft Wondrous Item, *alarm*, *light*, *mage's faithful hound*, *unseen servant*

LUMINOUS LOCKPICKS	PRICE 6,000 GP	
SLOT none	**CL** 3rd	**WEIGHT** 2 lbs.
AURA faint transmutation		

This set of fine, masterwork thieves' tools glimmer when exposed to light. When held in hand, they glow with light visible only to the individual holding them. This light allows the holder to work in all manners of darkness, including magical darkness, unimpeded and without attracting the attention of other creatures. This light does not provide enough illumination to see anything beyond a single lock or similar device on which the tools are used. As they glow, the tools vary their color, indicating favorable or unfavorable positioning within a device. These guiding lights grant a +5 circumstance bonus on Disable Device checks.

CONSTRUCTION REQUIREMENTS	COST 3,000 GP

Craft Wondrous Item, *knock*

PALELIGHT TORCH	PRICE 250 GP	
SLOT none	**CL** 2nd	**WEIGHT** 1 lb.
AURA faint evocation		

This torch is made from a dull, gray wood that bears intricate carvings. It burns like a normal torch, but only gives off dim light in a 40-foot radius. In areas of normal light, the torch reduces the light level to dim. The torch has no effect in areas of bright light.

CONSTRUCTION REQUIREMENTS	COST 125 GP

Craft Wondrous Item, *light*

RADIANT PANEL	PRICE 12,000 GP	
SLOT none	**CL** 5th	**WEIGHT** —
AURA faint evocation		

This small glass cube bears shallow indents carved into each side. Pressing an indentation as a standard action creates a thin sheet of hard light that is 5 feet wide. The sheet covers one edge of a 5-foot square, chosen at activation. While active, the sheet blocks attacks as if it is a solid wall, granting total cover against attacks and spells that pass through this edge. The sheet has hardness 10 and 30 hp. Force effects bypass this sheet, acting normally. The edge chosen can even be a horizontal one, creating a platform that can hold 500 pounds of weight.

Once active, the cube anchors itself in place, preventing the sheet from moving. Moving the cube while it is active requires a successful DC 22 Strength check. If the cube moves or if more than 500 pounds of weight is added to the sheet, the sheet shatters, requiring another activation to create a new sheet.

Light sheets created by the cube remain for 1 minute and a cube can create up to 5 sheets per day. A sheet can be dismissed as a standard action, expending the full use of that sheet.

CONSTRUCTION REQUIREMENTS	COST 6,000 GP

Craft Wondrous Item, *floating disk*

Shadowcraft Weapons

Although normally insubstantial, shadows can be crafted into semi-real shadowcraft items using a combination of illusion and necromancy. The resulting objects are almost exclusively used as weaponry, as the quasi-real nature of shadowcrafted substance makes it ill-suited for protection, and the necromantic powers at play result in vicious weapons whose animating force all but begs to sip the essence of living creatures.

The following *shadowcraft weapon* is the most basic of its kind. More advanced weaponry with additional powers and abilities are detailed below.

SHADOWCRAFT WEAPON		PRICE 12,500 GP
SLOT none	CL 10th	WEIGHT varies
AURA moderate illusion		

This highly malleable weapon is forged from insubstantial darkness using a combination of illusion and transmutation magic. Each *shadowcraft weapon* is designed with a base type (melee or ranged) and handedness (one-handed or two-handed for ranged weapons, and light, one-handed, or two-handed for melee weapons). Ranged *shadowcraft weapons* that use ammunition create their own projectiles out of shadow, but they can be loaded with and fire other types of ammunition, as well.

The wielder of a *shadowcraft weapon* can alter the weapon's shape as a standard action simply by picturing the form she wishes it to assume. A *shadowcraft weapon* can assume the form of any masterwork weapon that shares its type and handedness, regardless of its categorization as simple, martial, or exotic. *Shadowcraft weapons* are able to take the shape of weapons of different size categories, as long as they would be treated as the appropriate level of handedness for the *shadowcraft weapon's* true size. For example, a Medium two-handed melee *shadowcraft weapon* can become a greatsword sized for a Medium creature, or a longsword sized for a Large creature (which a Medium creature would treat as a two-handed weapon).

Shadowcraft weapons are quasi-real and deal less damage if an opponent realizes this. The first time each round that a creature is hit with a *shadowcraft weapon*, that creature can attempt a Will saving throw to disbelieve (DC = 15 + twice the weapon's enhancement bonus, if any). On a failed check, the weapon deals damage normally. On a successful save, all of the weapon's attacks against that creature do minimum damage until the wielder's next turn, and that creature gains a +4 bonus on subsequent saving throws to disbelieve the attacks of that wielder's *shadowcraft weapon*. *Shadowcraft weapons* deal only 1 point of damage to objects. In addition, the wielder of a *shadowcraft weapon* gains a +1 bonus on attack rolls and adds +1 to the save DC to disbelieve the attack if the opponent is in an area of dim light or darkness. In contrast, the wielder takes a −1 penalty on attack rolls and to the save DC to disbelieve the attack if the opponent is in an area of bright light.

A *shadowcraft weapon* can be enhanced like any other masterwork weapon and it retains all of its abilities between transformations, including enhancement bonuses and weapon special abilities, except those prohibited by its current shape. For example, a *keen shadowcraft weapon* functions normally in the form of a piercing or slashing weapon, but cannot use the *keen* special ability while in the shape of a bludgeoning weapon. A *shadowcraft weapon* retains the last appearance it was commanded to assume until its wielder commands it to assume a different form.

CONSTRUCTION REQUIREMENTS	COST 6,250 GP

Craft Magical Arms and Armor, *major creation*, *shadow weapon*^{UM}

Advanced Shadowcraft Weapons

The following advanced weapons build upon the malleable nature of shadowcraft weaponry by adding additional powers, abilities, and bonuses to those listed above. Like standard *shadowcraft weapons*, the following weapons can be further enhanced. If an advanced *shadowcraft weapon* doesn't note a specific handedness or weapon type, it can be created as a weapon of any handedness or weapon type of the crafter's choice.

ENERVATIVE SHADOWCRAFT WEAPON		PRICE 36,000 GP
SLOT none	CL 12th	WEIGHT varies
AURA strong illusion and necromancy		

This *shadowcraft weapon* glows with palpable malice, its hunger ceaselessly gnawing upon the wits of its wielder. Whenever the wielder of an *enervative shadowcraft weapon* confirms a critical hit with the weapon against an opponent that failed its Will saving throw to disbelieve, the opponent gains 1 negative level. One day after being struck, a target must succeed at a Fortitude saving throw (DC = 15 + the weapon's enhancement bonus, if any) for each negative level gained or any such levels become permanent.

CONSTRUCTION REQUIREMENTS	COST 18,000 GP

Craft Magic Arms and Armor, *enervation*, *major creation*, *shadow weapon*^{UM}

FOCUSED SHADOWCRAFT WEAPON		PRICE 13,000 GP
SLOT none	CL 12th	WEIGHT varies
AURA strong illusion		

This *melee shadowcraft weapon* is designed to act as a conduit for shadow magic, enhancing a spell's potency when the weapon is involved in its casting. As a swift action, a *focused shadowcraft weapon* can be used to increase the caster level of any spell of the shadow subschool or spell with the darkness or shadow^{UM} descriptors by 1.

CONSTRUCTION REQUIREMENTS	COST 6,500 GP

Craft Magic Arms and Armor, *imbue with spell ability*, *major creation*, *shadow weapon*^{UM}

LASHING SHADOWCRAFT WEAPON	PRICE 14,500 GP	
SLOT none	**CL** 10th	**WEIGHT** varies
AURA moderate illusion and transmutation		

This *two-handed melee shadowcraft weapon* is extremely ductile, and it easily bends and stretches without hampering its ability to harm opponents. On command, a *lashing shadowcraft weapon* can be extended as a swift action, increasing the weapon's reach by 5 feet for 1 round. While extended, the wielder does not threaten adjacent creatures, or creatures up to 10 feet away if the weapon already has reach.

CONSTRUCTION REQUIREMENTS	COST 7,250 GP

Craft Magic Arms and Armor, *long arm*ACG, *major creation*, *shadow weapon*UM

Divine Shadowcraft Weapons

The following shadowcraft weapons are tied to specific deities that grant the Darkness domain. While any character can wield them, the churches of the deities to which they are connected often see them as holy relics.

FEAST OF RATS	PRICE 45,125 GP	
SLOT none	**CL** 19th	**WEIGHT** varies
AURA strong evocation and illusion		

A swarm of shadowy rats clump together to form this *+1 stalking*UE *light melee shadowcraft weapon*. Three times per day, the wielder can throw the weapon into one square within 10 feet while speaking a command word, causing the weapon to disperse into a shadowy haze that functions as *fog cloud*. Each round, any creature within the *fog cloud* takes 1d6 points of damage and must succeed at a DC 19 Fortitude saving throw or become nauseated for 1 round. This effect lasts for 1 minute, after which the weapon returns to its previous form. Alternatively, any time before the effect's duration ends, the wielder can spend a move action while adjacent to the *fog cloud* to return the weapon to its previous form, dismissing the effect and returning the weapon to her hand.

A *feast of rats* can be used as an unholy symbol divine focus of Lao Shu Po, the Old Rat Woman.

CONSTRUCTION REQUIREMENTS	COST 22,712 GP

Craft Magical Arms and Armor, Create Reliquary Arms and ShieldsUM, *deeper darkness*, *fog cloud*, *major creation*, *shadow weapon*UM

TORMENT OF THE MIDNIGHT LORD	PRICE 60,000 GP	
SLOT none	**CL** 19th	**WEIGHT** varies
AURA strong illusion and necromancy		

This *+1 vicious two-handed melee shadowcraft weapon* has the texture and consistency of coagulated blood. A shadowy, chained skull always features prominently upon it regardless of what form a *torment of the Midnight Lord* assumes. Any creature suffering a bleed effect takes a penalty on Will saving throws to disbelieve the weapon's attacks equal to half the bleed damage the creature took on its last turn. In addition,

all damage dealt to a foe by the *vicious* weapon special ability of a *torment of the Midnight Lord* in any illumination condition other than bright light doesn't heal naturally and resists magical healing. A character attempting to use magical healing on a creature damaged by a *torment of the Midnight Lord* must succeed at a DC 21 caster level check, or the healing has no effect on the injured creature. Damage done to the wielder of a *torment of the Midnight Lord* does not have this effect, and can be healed normally.

A *torment of the Midnight Lord* can be used as an unholy symbol divine focus of Zon-Kuthon.

CONSTRUCTION REQUIREMENTS	COST 30,000 GP

Craft Magical Arms and Armor, Create Reliquary Arms and ShieldsUM, *major creation*, *shadow weapon*UM, *symbol of pain*

Shadow Feats

The following feats represent special tricks and abilities that characters who cling to the shadows can learn to boost their effectiveness. They grant abilities and benefits revolving around fighting and manipulating darkness and dim light.

Blinded Blade Style (Combat, Style)
You hold no fear of blindness, as your other senses improve without the distractions of sight.

Prerequisites: Blind-Fight, Perception 5 ranks.

Benefit: While you are using this style, you gain a number of benefits whenever you are blinded or unable to see (including when you wear a blindfold or close your eyes). Under such circumstances, you do not take any penalties on Strength- or Dexterity-based skill checks due to blindness. In addition, you gain a +4 bonus on hearing- and smell-based Perception checks and gain the scent special ability with a range of 10 feet; if you already have scent, the range of your scent ability increases by 10 feet instead. Having this feat counts as having 10 ranks in Perception for the purpose of satisfying the prerequisites of the Improved Blind-Fight[APG] feat, as well as any feat that lists Improved Blind-Fight[APG] as a prerequisite.

Blinded Competence (Combat)
Your lack of sight enables you to strike your foes with uncanny precision.

Prerequisites: Blinded Blade Style, Blind-Fight, Improved Blind-Fight[APG], Perception 10 ranks.

Benefit: While you are using Blinded Blade Style and you are blinded or unable to see, you do not need to succeed at Perception checks to pinpoint the location of creatures within reach of your melee weapon, or your unmodified reach if you are not wielding a melee weapon. This ability functions like blindsense, except creatures you cannot see do not gain total concealment against you. Having this feat counts as having 15 ranks in Perception for the purpose of satisfying the prerequisites of the Greater Blind-Fight[APG] feat, as well as any feat that lists Greater Blind-Fight[APG] as a prerequisite.

Blinded Master (Combat)
Your skill at arms while unable to see is astounding.

Prerequisites: Blind-Fight, Blinded Blade Precision, Blinded Blade Style, Greater Blind-Fight[APG], Improved Blind-Fight[APG], Perception 15 ranks.

Benefit: While you are using Blinded Blade Style and you are blinded or unable to see, your ability to pinpoint creatures' locations using Blinded Competence improves to function like blindsight rather than blindsense, and the range increases to 30 feet. In addition, you add half your character level to the DCs of Bluff checks to feint you in combat.

Cloak and Dagger Style (Combat, Style)
Your attacks effortlessly inflict debilitating conditions on unaware opponents.

Prerequisites: Int 13, Combat Expertise, Improved Dirty Trick[APG], Vital Strike, Weapon Focus with the chosen weapon, base attack bonus +6.

Benefit: Choose one light melee weapon. While using this style, whenever you use the attack action to attack an opponent during a surprise round with your chosen weapon, you can attempt a dirty trick[APG] combat maneuver check against that opponent as a free action. Additionally, if an adjacent target attempts to remove a condition that you inflicted upon it with the dirty trick combat maneuver, it provokes an attack of opportunity from you.

Special: In addition to the chosen weapon, a character with the weapon training class feature can use Cloak and Dagger Style with any light melee weapon belonging to any fighter weapon group he has selected with weapon training. A character with the swashbuckler weapon training[ACG] class feature can use Cloak and Dagger Style with light and one-handed piercing weapons.

Cloak and Dagger Subterfuge (Combat)

Your increased martial skill allows you to take advantage of distracted foes to easily impose conditions, and even steal items without being noticed.

Prerequisites: Int 13, Cloak and Dagger Style, Combat Expertise, Improved Dirty Trick[APG], Weapon Focus with the chosen weapon, base attack bonus +11.

Benefit: While you are using Cloak and Dagger Style and wielding your chosen weapon, whenever you make an attack of opportunity against a target, you can attempt a free dirty trick[APG] combat maneuver check against the target as a free action as well. Additionally, whenever you successfully perform a dirty trick maneuver against a target, you can immediately attempt a steal[APG] combat maneuver check against the target as a free action. If you succeed, the target is unaware you have stolen an item.

Cloak and Dagger Tactics (Combat)

You devastate enemies that you catch off-guard.

Prerequisites: Int 13, Cloak and Dagger Style, Cloak and Dagger Subterfuge, Combat Expertise, Improved Dirty Trick[APG], Vital Strike, Weapon Focus with the chosen weapon, base attack bonus +16.

Benefit: While you are using Cloak and Dagger Style and wielding your chosen weapon, whenever you hit an opponent that is denied its Dexterity bonus to AC or that you are flanking, or make an attack using Vital Strike (or its improved or greater versions), you can attempt a dirty trick[APG] combat maneuver check against that opponent as a free action. If you succeed, the target must succeed at a Fortitude save (DC = 10 + 1/2 your base attack bonus + your Intelligence modifier) or take an additional penalty from the dirty trick selected from the following list: anchored in place and unable to move from that square, confused, exhausted, or staggered. This additional penalty lasts only 1 round, regardless of how long the dirty trick's normal penalty lasts, and can be removed by the target with a standard action. You can only attempt one free dirty trick combat maneuver check per round using this feat.

Eclipsed Spell (Metamagic)

You alter how your spells affect illumination.

Benefit: Only spells that create areas of light or darkness can be eclipsed spells. If the eclipsed spell creates an area that shines like a torch or raises the light level by one step, you can choose to have the spell lower the illumination level in the affected area by one step, functioning like *darkness*. If the eclipsed spell creates an area that shines like daylight or raises the light level by two steps, you can choose to have the spell lower the illumination level in the affected area by two steps and create an area of magical darkness, functioning like *deeper darkness*.

If the eclipsed spell lowers the illumination level in the affected area by one step, you can choose to have the spell cause the affected area to glow with normal light, functioning like *light*. If the eclipsed spell lowers the illumination level in the affected area by two steps, you can choose to have the spell cause the affected area to shed bright light, functioning like *daylight*.

An eclipsed spell does not use up a higher-level spell slot than the spell's actual level.

Extra Ninja Trick

You have honed your shadowy skills further than most.

Prerequisite: Ninja trick[UC] class feature.

Benefit: You gain one additional ninja trick. You must meet all of the prerequisites for this ninja trick.

Special: You can gain Extra Ninja Trick multiple times.

Extra Shadow Jump

You have an improved ability to leap through shadow.

Prerequisite: Shadow jump shadowdancer class feature.

Benefit: Add 10 feet to the total distance you can jump each day using the shadow jump ability. The extra distance provided by this feat doubles whenever the distance that you can jump doubles (20 feet at 6th, 40 feet at 8th, and 80 feet at 10th level).

Special: This feat can be selected up to four times. Its effects stack.

Flexible Shadow Jump

You have refined your ability to leap through the shadows.

Prerequisite: Shadow jump shadowdancer class feature.

Benefit: When you travel between shadows using the shadow jump ability, the minimum increment that you can jump is 5 feet, allowing you to split your shadow jumps into 5-foot increments instead of 10-foot increments. In addition, your shadow jump ability counts as the ability to cast *dimension door* for the purpose of meeting the prerequisites of the Dimensional Agility[UC] feat as well as any feat that lists that feat as a prerequisite, and your shadow jump benefits from such feats as if you were casting *dimension door*.

Normal: Each shadow jump, no matter how small, counts as a 10-foot increment.

Snuffing Spell (Metamagic)

Your magic disrupts sources of light.

Benefit: You can modify a spell to extinguish magical and nonmagical light sources that the target has. The first time a creature takes damage from or fails a saving throw against a snuffing spell, any nonmagical light sources it has are immediately extinguished and you can attempt to dispel any active spells with the light descriptor that are affecting the target as if you had also cast the targeted version of *dispel magic*. Spells that do not target creatures can't be snuffing spells.

A snuffing spell uses up a spell slot 2 levels higher than the spell's actual level.

Shadow Magic Items

Creatures that dwell in darkness tend to favor magic items that spread shadows and banish light. Many of the items below allow the wielder to cast her enemies into penumbral terror before delivering the final blow.

ECLIPSED METAMAGIC ROD		PRICE varies
Lesser eclipsed metamagic rod		1,500 GP
Eclipsed metamagic rod		5,500 GP
Greater eclipsed metamagic rod		12,250 GP
SLOT none	**CL** 17th	**WEIGHT** 5 lbs.
AURA strong (no school)		

The wielder can cast up to three spells per day that alter how the spell raises or lowers the illumination level in their affected areas as though using the Eclipsed Spell feat (see page 25).

CONSTRUCTION REQUIREMENTS	COST varies
Lesser eclipsed metamagic rod	750 GP
Eclipsed metamagic rod	2,750 GP
Greater eclipsed metamagic rod	6,125 GP

Craft Rod, Eclipsed Spell

EYE-STEALING LOCKET		PRICE 24,000 GP
SLOT none	**CL** 3rd	**WEIGHT** —
AURA faint necromancy		

This silver locket is suspended from a silver chain. As a standard action, a creature holding the locket can speak a command word to attempt to steal the sight of one creature within 30 feet. The target must succeed at a DC 13 Fortitude saving throw or its eyes are immediately sealed within the locket's interior and replaced with featureless, shadowy orbs, causing the creature to be permanently blinded. The wielder can speak a second command word to return the victim's eyes; otherwise, this blindness cannot be removed except by *miracle* or *wish*.

Each *eye-stealing locket* can contain only a single set of eyes at a time, and the creature in possession of the locket is treated as having a body part of the creature to whom the eyes belong for the purpose of spells such as *scrying*. If the wielder is a mesmerist and he uses an *eye-stealing locket* against the target of his hypnotic stare, he can apply the Will saving throw penalty from his hypnotic stare to the Fortitude saving throw the target attempts to prevent its eyes being stolen.

CONSTRUCTION REQUIREMENTS	COST 12,000 GP
Craft Wondrous Item, *blindness/deafness*

ROD OF DELUMINATION		PRICE 35,000 GP
SLOT none	**CL** 17th	**WEIGHT** 5 lbs.
AURA strong evocation		

This silvery rod is spoon-sized and utterly featureless. A creature holding a *rod of delumination* can extinguish any ability, item, or spell effect that is acting as a light source simply by pointing one end of the rod at the light and uttering a command word.

Sources of magical light receive a DC 15 Will saving throw to negate this effect and have a Will save bonus equal to half their caster level; if the original caster of the effect is still within the spell's range, the spell can use its caster's Will save bonus instead. If a light source succeeds at its saving throw against a *rod of delumination*, the same rod cannot affect it again for 24 hours. No other properties of an affected creature, item, or spell are altered other than its ability to shed light; a torch continues to burn, a lantern continues to consume oil, and so on.

The bearer can, if she chooses, utter a second command word to reignite any light source the rod has previously extinguished, provided that the light source's normal duration hasn't expired.

CONSTRUCTION REQUIREMENTS	COST 17,500 GP
Craft Rod, Snuffing Spell (see page 25)

SHADOWBOND TUNIC		PRICE 12,000 GP
SLOT chest	**CL** 3rd	**WEIGHT** 5 lbs.
AURA faint abjuration		

This black linen tunic has simple brass buttons. Once per day, the wielder can attune the garment to one ally by standing for 1 minute in a position in which both the wielder's and his ally's shadows overlap. For the next 24 hours, whenever the wielder is adjacent to that ally and that ally takes damage, the wielder can sacrifice up to 10 hit points to prevent an equal amount of damage done to the ally. This damage cannot be reduced or redirected, and if the wielder is incapable of sacrificing hit points, the damage to the ally cannot be prevented. If the vest is removed before its duration ends, the connection between the wielder and ally is lost and the vest is powerless until 24 hours have passed since its last attunement.

CONSTRUCTION REQUIREMENTS	COST 6,000 GP
Craft Wondrous Item, *shield other*

SHADOWSHOOTING		PRICE +1 bonus
SLOT none	**CL** 8th	**WEIGHT** —
AURA moderate conjuration		

This special ability can only be added to ranged projectile weapons (including slings and sling-like weapons). Black smoke constantly wafts from the firing mechanism of a *shadowshooting* weapon. A *shadowshooting* weapon never needs to be reloaded; after a shot is fired, this smoke immediately coalesces into the ammunition required to fire the weapon again. This doesn't prevent a *shadowshooting* weapon from firing ordinary projectiles appropriate to the weapon.

Ammunition created by this ability is only quasi-real, and the first time each round an opponent is hit by a piece of ammunition that this ability has created, it can attempt a Will saving throw to disbelieve (DC = 15 + the weapon's enhancement bonus). A failed Will saving throw means the weapon deals damage normally, while success means the weapon deals minimum damage against that opponent for 1 round.

CONSTRUCTION REQUIREMENTS	COST +1 bonus

Craft Magical Arms and Armor, *reloading hands*[UC], *shadow weapon*[UM]

SHAWL OF SHADOWY DISGUISE		PRICE 1,350 GP
SLOT head	**CL** 5th	**WEIGHT** 1 lb.
AURA faint illusion		

This violet shawl twists and melds with the darkness, becoming as black as coal in even the faintest shadow. While worn, the wearer can hide her appearance as if with a *penumbral disguise* spell (see page 29). Onlookers never discern that the wearer was wearing a *shawl of shadowy disguise*.

CONSTRUCTION REQUIREMENTS	COST 675 GP

Craft Wondrous Item, *penumbral disguise*

SNUFFING METAMAGIC ROD		PRICE varies
Lesser snuffing metamagic rod		9,000 GP
Snuffing metamagic rod		32,500 GP
Greater snuffing metamagic rod		73,000 GP
SLOT none	**CL** 17th	**WEIGHT** 5 lbs.
AURA strong (no school)		

The wielder can cast up to three spells per day that extinguish magical and nonmagical sources of light active on the target as though using the Snuffing Spell feat (see page 25).

CONSTRUCTION REQUIREMENTS	COST varies
Lesser snuffing metamagic rod	4,500 GP
Snuffing metamagic rod	16,250 GP
Greater snuffing metamagic rod	36,500 GP

Craft Rod, Snuffing Spell

SOLES OF THE SILENT STRIDE		PRICE 8,250 GP
SLOT feet	**CL** 3rd	**WEIGHT** —
AURA faint transmutation		

These simple leather shoes are the color of a moonless night and instantly adjust to the wearer's foot shape, becoming skintight while providing magical cushioning and support. The wearer gains a +5 competence bonus on Stealth checks and can attempt Stealth checks while running at a −20 penalty.

CONSTRUCTION REQUIREMENTS	COST 4,125 GP

Craft Wondrous Item, *silence*

TOME OF DISSOLUTION		PRICE 2,000 GP
SLOT none	**CL** 5th	**WEIGHT** 1 lb.
AURA faint illusion		

This shadowy, waterproof tome is 12 inches tall, 8 inches wide, and 1 inch thick. When viewed in dim, normal, or bright light, the tome's 1,000 ebon pages are blank and any new writing immediately fades from sight, as if *erase* had been cast upon the page. When viewed in darkness, however, each page becomes outlined with pale, silvery light and anything then written in the tome is recorded in similar, silvery light. Writings within the tome are protected as per *nondetection*. A *tome of*

dissolution can be used as a formula book or a spellbook; if so, extracts and spells can only be prepared from the tome when viewed in darkness. Necromancy spells, spells of the shadow subschool, and spells with the darkness or shadow[UM] descriptor take half as many pages when copied into a *tome of dissolution* as they would in a normal spellbook or formula book.

CONSTRUCTION REQUIREMENTS	COST 1,000 GP

Craft Wondrous Item, *erase, nondetection, secret page*

VOIDLIGHT LANTERN		PRICE 30,000 GP
SLOT none	**CL** 5th	**WEIGHT** 2 lbs.
AURA faint evocation		

This ornately designed lantern is crafted from volcanic glass. When lit, the lantern's magic creates an area of darkness in a 20-foot radius and lowers the illumination level by one step for an additional 20 feet beyond that area (bright light becomes normal light, normal light becomes dim light, and dim light becomes darkness). If used in an area of darkness, a *voidlight lantern* creates an area of supernatural darkness (as per *deeper darkness*) in a 20-foot radius instead.

CONSTRUCTION REQUIREMENTS	COST 15,000 GP

Craft Wondrous Item, *deeper darkness*

Penumbral Spells

Although many think of shadow and light as utterly separate elements, penumbral spellcasters understand that darkness and light are like hot and cold or life and death—two extremes of the same concept, each meaningless without the other. As a result, many spellcasters who dabble in darkness pay equal homage to the light, for the ability to manipulate one is practically worthless without the ability to command the other.

DANCING DARKNESS

School evocation [darkness, shadow^{UM}]; **Level** antipaladin 1, bard 1, magus 1, shaman 1, psychic 1, sorcerer/wizard 1, spiritualist 1, witch 1
Casting Time 1 standard action
Components V, S
Range medium (100 ft. + 10 ft./level)
Effect Up to four spheres, all within a 10-ft.-radius area
Duration 1 minute/level (D)
Saving Throw none; **Spell Resistance** no

You create either up to four spheres of darkness that each reduce the illumination level by one step within a 20-foot-radius, or one dimly lit, vaguely humanoid shape. Each sphere of *dancing darkness* must stay within a 10-foot-radius area of one another but can otherwise move as you desire (no concentration required): forward or back, up or down, straight or turning corners, or the like. The darkness can move up to 100 feet per round. The effect winks out if the distance between you and it exceeds the spell's range.

Dancing shadows can be made permanent with a *permanency* spell.

MOTES OF DUSK AND DAWN

School evocation [darkness, light]; **Level** bard 3, magus 3, medium 3, mesmerist 3, occultist 3, psychic 3, shaman 3, sorcerer/wizard 3, witch 3
Casting Time 1 standard action
Components V, S
Range medium (100 ft. + 10 ft./level)
Effect Up to four motes, all within a 10-ft.-radius area
Duration 1 minute (D)
Saving Throw none; **Spell Resistance** no

When you cast this spell, you create up to four motes that shed light or darkness in a 20-foot-radius, increasing or decreasing the illumination level by up to two categories. You decide whether each individual mote sheds light or darkness when the spell is cast.

The *motes of dusk and dawn* must stay within a 10-foot-radius area of one another but otherwise move as you desire (no concentration required): forward or back, up or down, straight or turning corners, or the like. The motes can move up to 100 feet per round. A mote winks out if the distance between you and it exceeds the spell's range.

MYDRIATIC SPONTANEITY

School evocation [darkness, light]; **Level** bard 3, mesmerist 3, psychic 3, sorcerer/wizard 4, witch 4
Casting Time 1 standard action
Components V, S
Range close (25 ft. + 5 ft./2 levels)
Targets one living creature
Duration 1 round/level
Saving Throw Will negates; **Spell Resistance** yes

You overstimulate the target with alternating flashes of light and shadow within its eyes, causing its pupils to rapidly dilate and contract. While under the effects of this spell, the target is racked by splitting headaches and unable to see clearly, becoming nauseated for the spell's duration. Each round, the target's pupils randomly become dilated or contracted for 1 round. During any round that its eyes are dilated, the target is blinded if exposed to bright light or dazzled if exposed to normal light. During any round its eyes are contracted, the target is blinded if exposed to darkness or dazzled if exposed to dim light. In addition, any creature can attempt a Stealth check to avoid detection from the target, even if the creature lacks cover or concealment.

MYDRIATIC SPONTANEITY, MASS

School evocation [darkness, light]; **Level** bard 5, mesmerist 5, psychic 6, sorcerer/wizard 7, witch 7

Targets one or more living creatures, no two of which can be more than 30 ft. apart

This spell functions as *mydriatic spontaneity*, except it can affect multiple creatures.

PENUMBRAL DISGUISE

School conjuration [shadow^UM]; **Level** alchemist 3, bard 3, inquisitor 3, mesmerist 3, occultist 3, sorcerer/wizard 3, witch 3

Casting Time 1 standard action

Components V, S

Range touch

Target creature touched

Duration 10 minutes/level (D)

Saving Throw none; **Spell Resistance** no

You mask your features with shadowy illumination, gaining a competence bonus equal to your caster level on Disguise checks and Stealth checks attempted while in normal light, dim light, or darkness. In addition, creatures that see you while you are in dim light or darkness are unable to discern any but the most general information about your appearance or actions. For example, they can determine your general shape (such as humanoid), as well as the gist of your actions (such as, "She was trying to break into the store"), but cannot determine your precise actions, your appearance, or any identifying information about you. In bright light, your normal appearance is revealed.

SHIELD OF DARKNESS

School evocation [darkness, shadow^UM]; **Level** antipaladin 3, cleric 3, inquisitor 3, shaman 3, spiritualist 3

Casting Time 1 standard action

Components V

Range personal

Target you

Duration 1 round/level (D)

Saving Throw none; **Spell Resistance** no

You shield yourself with darkness, reducing the illumination level in your space to magical darkness and granting you total concealment. Your opponents are automatically aware of which squares you occupy, preventing you from attempting Stealth checks using this concealment unless every square adjacent to you has an illumination level of darkness or lower. *Shield of darkness* does not hinder your vision, and creatures that can see in magical darkness ignore this effect.

SPOTLIGHT

School evocation [darkness, light]; **Level** bard 3, cleric 3, druid 3, inquisitor 3, magus 3, occultist 3, paladin 3, shaman 3, sorcerer/wizard 3, witch 3

Casting Time 1 standard action

Components V, S

Range long (400 ft. + 40 ft./level)

Target one creature

Duration 1 minute/level (D)

Saving Throw Reflex partial; **Spell Resistance** yes

You create a mobile area of bright light centered on one target while simultaneously suppressing other light sources surrounding it. The light level in the target's space increases to bright light, causing the target to take any penalties that it would normally take in bright light. In addition, all mundane light sources (and magic light sources of 3rd spell level or lower) within 20 feet of the target's space are suppressed, shedding no light as long as they remain within this spell's affected area and reverting the area normally affected by those light sources to their unmodified illumination levels.

The effects of spotlight are centered on the target and move as the target does. As a result, the target takes a −20 penalty on all Stealth checks for the spell's duration and cannot benefit from concealment normally provided by darkness, as though illuminated with *faerie fire*.

If the target succeeds at its Reflex save, the spotlight is created in the target's square but does not move with the target, and it hinders the Stealth checks only of creatures within that square.

TOUCH OF BLINDNESS

School necromancy [darkness, shadow^UM]; **Level** antipaladin 1, bard 1, cleric 1, sorcerer/wizard 1, shaman 1, witch 1

Casting Time 1 standard action

Components V

Range touch

Target creature or creatures touched (up to one/level)

Duration 1 round/level (see text)

Saving Throw Fortitude negates; **Spell Resistance** Yes

A touch from your hand, which is engulfed in darkness, disrupts a creature's vision by coating its eyes in supernatural darkness. Each touch causes the target to become blinded for 1 round unless it makes a successful Fortitude saving throw. You can use this melee touch attack up to one time per caster level. Any touch attack not used after 1 round per caster level is lost.

WALL OF SPLIT ILLUMINATION

School evocation [darkness, light]; **Level** bard 3, cleric 3, sorcerer/wizard 3, inquisitor 3, magus 3, occultist 3, shaman 3

Casting Time 1 standard action

Components V, S

Range medium (100 ft. + 10 ft./level)

Effect 10-ft.-high vertical sheet of illumination up to 5 ft. long/level

Duration 1 minute/level (D)

Saving Throw none; **Spell Resistance** no

An immobile curtain of illumination springs into existence. When created, one side of the wall (designated by you) radiates bright light to a range of 60 feet away from that side while the other side radiates darkness to an equal distance. This effect alters the illumination level by up to two steps toward either bright light (the light side) or darkness (the dark side). The wall also obstructs vision through it, regardless of which side of the wall the viewer is on.

Shadow Spells

Whereas the shadows that permeate the Material Plane merely denote the absence of light, the darkness of the Shadow Plane is in part created by the Negative Energy Plane. The Shadow Plane is home to beings and structures twisted by this influence into pale, quasi-real reflections of true creatures and objects native to the Material Plane. Closely tied to the forces that animate undead and abounding with phantasmal figments, shadow magic is heavily associated with the schools of illusion and necromancy. The following new spells use the energy of the Shadow Plane to fuel their effects.

BALEFUL SHADOW TRANSMUTATION

School illusion (shadow) [shadow^UM]; **Level** alchemist 6, bard 6, druid 7, medium 6, shaman 6, sorcerer/wizard 6, spiritualist 6, summoner 6, witch 6

Casting Time 1 standard action

Components V, S

Range close (25 ft. + 5 ft./2 levels)

Target one creature

Duration permanent

Saving Throw Will disbelief, then Fortitude negates; **Spell Resistance** yes

You infuse a target's shadow with energies from the Shadow Plane, shaping the shadow into one that appears to belong to a different creature, and tricking the target into believing it actually is that creature. When you cast this spell, choose one Huge or smaller creature of the animal type or one Medium or Small creature of the humanoid type. If the chosen creature is ill suited to the target's current environment, such as an aquatic creature not in water, the subject gains a +4 bonus on all saving throws against *baleful shadow transmutation*. If the subject fails its Will save, it believes that it is the chosen creature, causing it to lose its extraordinary, supernatural, and spell-like abilities, lose its ability to cast spells (if it had the ability), and gain the alignment, special abilities, and Intelligence, Wisdom, and Charisma scores of its new form in place of its own. It retains any class features (other than spellcasting) that aren't extraordinary, supernatural, or spell-like abilities.

When the subject is first targeted by this spell, and once every 24 hours thereafter, the subject must attempt a Will save in order to disbelieve this effect. If the save succeeds, the spell's effect ends. The first time the subject fails this save, it must also attempt a Fortitude save. If it also fails this Fortitude save, the subject permanently assumes the form of the chosen animal or humanoid, as per *polymorph*. This is a polymorph effect. Successfully disbelieving the spell returns the subject to its true form. If the subject fails its Fortitude save against the effects of *baleful shadow transmutation*, any further polymorph effects cast on the target automatically fail.

Incorporeal or gaseous creatures are immune to *baleful shadow transmutation*, and a creature with the shapechanger subtype can revert to its natural form as a standard action.

MASOCHISTIC SHADOW

School necromancy [evil, shadow^UM]; **Level** antipaladin 4, bloodrager 4, magus 4, occultist 4, shaman 4, sorcerer/wizard 4, witch 4

Casting Time 1 standard action

Components V, S

Range close (25 ft. + 5 ft./level)

Target one creature

Duration 1 round/level (D)

Saving Throw Will negates, then Reflex partial; see text; **Spell Resistance** yes

You animate the target's shadow with semi-living energies drawn from the Shadow Plane, instilling a maddening hunger for its owner's life energy within it. If the target fails its Will save, it takes 1d4 points of Strength damage as a quasi-real shadow manifests in its space and attacks it. This shadow remains attached to the target and moves wherever the target moves.

At the start of each subsequent round, the target must succeed at a Reflex save or take 1d4 additional points of Strength damage; a successful save reduces the Strength damage to 1 point. If its Strength score is reduced to 0 by this spell's effects, the target dies. If the target is in bright light, it gains a +2 bonus on Reflex saves against this spell. If the target is in darkness, it takes a –2 penalty on Reflex saves against this spell.

SHADOW TRANSMUTATION

School illusion (shadow) [shadow^UM]; **Level** bard 6, medium 6, shaman 6, sorcerer/wizard 6, spiritualist 6, summoner 6, witch 6

Casting Time 1 standard action

Components V, S

Range see text

Target see text

Duration see text

Saving Throw Will disbelief (if interacted with); varies; see text; **Spell Resistance** yes; see text

You suffuse one subject's body with energy from the Shadow Plane, altering its form to match a creature from the Shadow Plane. Shadow transmutation can mimic any of the following spells: *animal growth, anthropomorphic animal^UM, enlarge person, fins to feet^ARG, longarm^ACG, polymorph, reduce person,* and *stone fist.* If using *shadow transmutation* as *polymorph*, the target does not gain any sensory abilities that its new form has (such as low-light vision or darkvision) and the speed of any movement types gained from the spell cannot exceed the target's base speed or natural speed with those movement types (whichever is higher). A creature under the effects of *shadow transmutation* deals normal damage and has all the normal abilities and weaknesses of whatever form it assumes using the spell.

Any creature that interacts with a target under the effects of the spell (including attacking or being attacked by that creature) can attempt a Will save to recognize the target's true nature. Creatures that succeed at their Will saves to disbelieve the illusion take one-fifth (20%) of the normal damage from the target's natural attacks or special abilities granted by the target's shadowy form (if any), and the target's special abilities that don't deal damage have only a 20% chance of working against them. Creatures that succeed at their saves see the *shadow transmutation* as transparent images superimposed over the target.

SHADOW TRANSMUTATION, GREATER

School illusion (shadow) [shadow^UM]; **Level** shaman 9, sorcerer/wizard 9, witch 9

This spell functions like *shadow transmutation*, except it can mimic *greater polymorph* instead of *polymorph*. The illusory attacks and special abilities of any shape assumed using *greater shadow transmutation* deal three-fifths (60%) damage to nonbelievers, and nondamaging effects are 60% likely to work against nonbelievers.

SHADOW TRAP

School illusion (shadow); **Level** antipaladin 1, bard 1, bloodrager 1, cleric 1, mesmerist 1, occultist 1, psychic 1, shaman 1, sorcerer/ wizard 1, witch 1

Casting Time 1 standard action

Components V, S

Range close (25 ft. + 5 ft./level)

Target one creature

Duration 1 round/level (D)

Saving Throw Will negates; **Spell Resistance** yes

You pin the target's shadow to its current location, causing the target to become entangled and preventing it from moving farther than 5 feet from its original position, as if its shadow were anchored to the terrain. Each round on its turn, the target can attempt a new saving throw to end the effect as a full-round action. A flying creature can only hover in place or fall while entangled in this manner. This spell automatically fails when cast on a creature that doesn't throw a shadow, and it ends if the creature is entirely in an area with no illumination.

SHADOWFORM

School illusion (shadow) [shadow^UM]; **Level** antipaladin 4, bard 4, mesmerist 4, psychic 4, sorcerer/wizard 4, spiritualist 4, witch 4

Casting Time 1 standard action

Components V, S

Range touch

Target creature touched

Duration 1 round/level (D)

Saving Throw Will negates (see text); **Spell Resistance** yes

You replace the target's body with mystic shadow material drawn from the Shadow Plane, rendering the target's physical form only quasi-real. Whenever a foe tries to directly attack the target of the spell (for instance, with a weapon or a targeted spell), that foe must attempt a Will save to disbelieve. If successful, the opponent can attack the target normally and is unaffected by *shadowform* for 1 round. If the foe fails, the target takes only one-fifth the normal amount of damage from the foe's successful attack or effect, and if the attack has a special effect other than damage, that effect is one-fifth as strong as normal (if applicable) or only 20% as likely to occur. Objects automatically succeed at their Will saves against this spell.

UMBRAL INFUSION

School necromancy [shadow^UM]; **Level** alchemist 4, antipaladin 4, cleric 4, occultist 4, psychic 4, shaman 4, sorcerer/wizard 4, witch 4

Casting Time 1 standard action

Components V, S

Range close (25 ft. + 5 ft./2 levels)

Target one mindless undead creature

Duration 1 minute/level

Saving Throw Will negates; **Spell Resistance** yes

You infuse the target mindless undead creature with power drawn from the Shadow Plane, immediately granting it the advanced creature simple template. It gains a +2 bonus on all rolls, including damage rolls, a +2 bonus to special ability DCs, a +4 bonus to AC and CMD, and 2 additional hit points per Hit Die. The undead creature's destructive instincts take hold for the duration of this spell, and any attempts to control or command the undead creature have a 50% chance of failing; if uncontrolled, the undead creature attacks any living creatures it sees. This spell has no effect on undead creatures that already have the advanced creature template.

UMBRAL INFUSION, MASS

School necromancy [shadow^UM]; **Level** cleric 8, sorcerer/wizard 8, witch 8

Target one mindless undead creature/level, no two of which can be more than 30 ft. apart

This spell functions as *umbral infusion*, except it can affect multiple mindless undead creatures.

Next Month!

The most experienced combatants know that the best offense is a good defense—and the best defense uses the secrets in *Pathfinder Player Companion: Armor Master's Handbook*! From shield style feats and advanced armor mastery to strategies for turning the weight and bulk of armor to your advantage, this guide to heavily armored heroics includes new options for every ironclad character, as well as combat tricks and a stamina system sure to see you through nearly any scrap unscathed.

Would You Like to Know More?

Those with the blood of shadows in their veins do more than just lurk in the gloom and plot to take down those who bask in the light. Learn more about how to live in the darkness with the following Pathfinder products that complement *Blood of Shadows*!

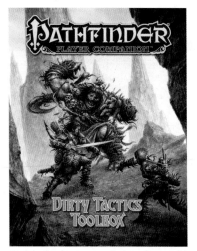

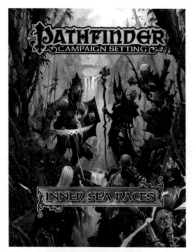

One advantage to being born in shadow is learning to cling to the darkness so your worst deeds go unseen. Pick up more nasty tricks to perform sneakily in *Pathfinder Player Companion: Dirty Tactics Toolbox*.

There's much more to know about drow, fetchlings, and wayangs and their insidious plots. Learn how these races interact with the rest of Golarion in *Pathfinder Campaign Setting: Inner Sea Races*.

If you take a wrong turn in the city of Magnimar, you'll find the Shadow, a district cloaked in constant gloom. Discover more about this area in *Pathfinder Campaign Setting: Magnimar, City of Monuments*.